AF746872

EGYPT'S ECONOMIC PREDICAMENT

SOCIAL, ECONOMIC AND POLITICAL STUDIES OF THE MIDDLE EAST

ÉTUDES SOCIALES, ÉCONOMIQUES ET POLITIQUES DU MOYEN ORIENT

Editor

C.A.O. van Nieuwenhuijze

Editorial Advisory Board

Samir Khalaf (Princeton University), M. Fathalla al-Khatib (Cairo University), Afaf Lutfi al-Sayyid Marsot (University of California at Los Angeles), Şerif Mardin (The American University, Washington DC), Udo Steinbach (Deutsches Orient Institut, Hamburg), Rodney Wilson (University of Durham)

VOLUME LI

EGYPT'S ECONOMIC PREDICAMENT

A Study in the Interaction of External Pressure, Political Folly and Social Tension in Egypt, 1960-1990

BY

GALAL A. AMIN

E.J. BRILL
LEIDEN · NEW YORK · KÖLN
1995

– 8 JUN 1998

338.962
Ami

The paper in this book meets the guidelines for permanence and durability of the Committee on Production Guidelines for Book Longevity of the Council on Library Resources.

Library of Congress Cataloging-in-Publication Data

Amin, Galal A., 1935–
Egypt's economic predicament : a study in the interaction of external pressure, political folly, and social tension in Egypt, 1960-1990 / by Galal A. Amin.
p. cm. — (Social, economic, and political studies of the Middle East, ISSN 0085–6193 ; v. 51)
Includes bibliographical references and index.
ISBN 9004101888
1. Structural adjustment (Economic policy)—Egypt. 2. Debts, External—Egypt. 3. Egypt—Economic conditions—1952– 4. Egypt–Social conditions—1952– 5. Egypt—Politics and government—1952– I. Title. II. Series.
HC830.A738 1995
338.962—dc20 94-46801
CIP

PK1372
AMI

Die Deutsche Bibliothek - CIP-Einheitsaufnahme

Amin, Ǧalāl A.:
Egypt's economic predicament : a study in the interaction of external pressure, political folly, and social tension in Egypt, 1960-1990 / by Gamal A. Amin. - Leiden ; New York ; Köln : Brill, 1995
(Social, economic, and political studies of the Middle East ; Vol. 51)
ISBN 90–04–10188–8
NE:GT

BAE 507

ISSN 0085-6193
ISBN 90 04 10188 8

© Copyright 1995 by E.J. Brill, Leiden, The Netherlands

All rights reserved. No part of this publication may be reproduced, translated, stored in a retrieval system, or transmitted in any form or by any means, electronic, mechanical, photocopying, recording or otherwise, without prior written permission from the publisher.

Authorization to photocopy items for internal or personal use is granted by E.J. Brill provided that the appropriate fees are paid directly to The Copyright Clearance Center, 222 Rosewood Drive, Suite 910 Danvers MA 01923, USA. Fees are subject to change.

PRINTED IN THE NETHERLANDS

For *Jan*
in gratitude for thirty years
of love and friendship

CONTENTS

PREFACE

For almost the whole of two decades (1970–1990), the problem of external debt continued to be one of the main preoccupations of policy makers and informed public opinion in Egypt. Throughout the 1980's, it was widely considered as Egypt's major economic problem. Having emerged as a consequence of persistent deficit in the balance of payments, by the mid 1980's it has become itself one of the major burdens on the balance of payments. It has also become, at least since the early 1980's, a major constraint on Egypt's freedom to take its own political decisions. To cope with the problem seemed to require action on all economic fronts, and the discussion of its causes evoked all the ailments of the Egyptian economy.

During the Gulf crisis of 1990/91, Egypt obtained an unexpected relief in the form of exemptions from a significant part of its external debt owed to some Arab Gulf states and to the United States. This was followed by other exemptions provided by country members of the Paris Club in May 1991. The latter exemptions, provided under the auspices of the IMF, were tied, however, to Egypt's compliance with the IMF and World Bank demands for stabilization measures and the implementation of a "structural adjustment" program. Egypt's progress in the implementation of those measures and program was to be reviewed and condoned before the last two reductions of the debt would be enforced, in November 1992 and May 1994. Egypt's economic policies have therefore been partly shaped by the demands of its creditors and will continue to be so until the debt burden is greatly reduced.

To discuss the causes of the emergence of Egypt's external debt in the early 1960's, and to follow its development during the subsequent three decades is virtually to inquire into the whole economic history of this period. To investigate the prospects of eliminating or greatly reducing the external debt, and the policy measures required to achieve this, amounts to an investigation of almost all the major aspects of Egypt's economic problem. The greater part of this book is the result of these investigations into the causes of the emergence and the development of Egypt's external debt (Chapter One), the causes and prospects of Egypt's performance with regard to the rates of saving and investment (Chapter Two), the prospects of the four major sources of foreign exchange, namely, oil, labour remittances, the Suez Canal and tourism (Chapter Three), and the performance and prospects of agriculture (Chapter Four) and manufacturing industry (Chapter Five). Chapter Six spells out the implications of the discussion of the previous chapters for the future of Egypt's external debt, and warns against the implications of "structural adjustment" which constitutes the conventional wisdom of today. The last two chapters try to bring the economic developments of Egypt during the last three decades into a wider historical perspective (Chapter Seven), and to trace their relationship with the emergence and growth of the phenomenon of religious fanaticism (Chapter Eight).

In writing this book I am indebted to many people. An earlier version of the first six chapters was the result of a research project performed under the auspices of the Arab Center for Development and Future Research in Cairo. I am grateful to its director, Mr. Gamil Mattar, for his continuous and generous support, as well as to the International Development Research Centre of Canada for its financial support of that earlier version of the book. I am also thankful to Dr. Sami El-Sayed, of the Faculty of Economics, Cairo University, and to Mrs. Ragaa Abdel Moneim, of the Research Department of the Central Bank of Egypt, for their assistance in this research project. I am particularly grateful to Dr. Philip English, Dr. Robinton Medhora and Dr. Fawzy Kishk, all of IDRC. None of these people is of course responsible for the final outcome or for the views expressed in this book. I would also like to thank Mrs. Nabila Boulos, of the Economic Department of the American University in Cairo, for her intelligent and efficient assistance in bringing this book to its final form.

On the 7th of June 1993, the ACDFR organized a symposium to discuss an earlier version of the first six chapters of this book. Ten prominent Egyptian economists as well as Dr. M. Medhora from IDRC, participated in a six-hour discussion. In choosing the names of invited economists from Egypt, the ACDFR tried to have an almost equal number of Egyptian economists known to be supporters of the structural adjustment program, which is criticized in this book, to those holding the opposite point of view, but high academic standing was the primary consideration. Thus, in addition to Dr. Medhora, participants included Gouda Abdel Khalek, of the Faculty of Economics, Cairo University, Ibrahim Helmy Abdel-Rahman, ex-Minister of Planning, Mohamed Abu Mandour, of the Faculty of Agriculture, Cairo University, Hazem El-Beblawy, Chairman of Export Development Bank of Egypt, Nadia Farah, Director of Arab Women Centre for Training and Research, Heba Handoussa, of the American University in Cairo, Hanaa Kheir El-Din, of the Faculty of Economics, Cairo University, Ibrahim Saad El-Din, of the Third World Forum, Cairo, Abdel-Aziz El-Sherbiny, of the Central Bank of Egypt, and Ramzi Zaki, of the National Planning Institute. Fawzy Kishk, Director of the IDRC Office in Cairo, and Gamil Mattar, Director of ACDFR, also participated. I found the discussion extremely valuable and many excellent points of criticism, qualification, addition and suggestions for improvement were made. In this final version I tried to incorporate and recognize as many of these points as I could, sometimes with and sometimes without approval. When I found the corrections or suggestions unquestionable I included them in the text, and when controversial I referred to them in footnotes. The book has certainly gained as a result, and I am again grateful for all the participants for the trouble they took to make the contents of those chapters which they read, closer to the truth.

Galal Amin
Cairo, 28 June 1994

LIST OF TABLES

TABLE

CHAPTER ONE

THE EMERGENCE AND DEVELOPMENT OF EGYPT'S EXTERNAL DEBT

1.1 *External Debt during Nasser's Five-Year Plan*

Fifty years ago, an important event took place in the history of Egypt's external debt, for in 1943, the long and rather depressing story of 19th-century indebtedness came to an end. The Second World War transferred Egypt from a debtor to a creditor country, mainly as a result of military expenditure of the Allies' troops in Egypt, and in 1943, whatever remained from its external debt was converted into a local one in which the creditors were either Egyptians or foreigners residing in Egypt. By the end of the war, Egypt had become a net creditor to Britain by no less than 430 million sterling pounds, a huge sum by the standards of that time.

For another 15 years, including the first seven years following the 1952 revolution, Egypt continued to be free of foreign debt. During those years Egypt did receive some foreign grants and even loans, but they were in small quantities and did not in any case require repayment in foreign currencies. American aid to Egypt during the early days of the revolution was either in the form of technical-assistance grants (according to the Point Four Program) or food aid according to P.L. 480, which was to be repaid in Egyptian currency. In fact, food aid to Egypt during that period did not exceed $17 million, which was given in one year (1955/56), and was not resumed until 1958/9.[1] Other than this, Egypt signed two loan agreements with the Soviet Union, one to finance the iron and steel complex in Helwan, and the other to finance the first stage of the High Dam (for $170 million and $97 million respectively), and another agreement for economic cooperation with West Germany for $124 million, but no disbursement was made from any of these three loans until the end of 1958.[2]

---

[1] Amin, G.: *Food Supply and Economic Development*, Cass, London, 1966, p. 90.

[2] Ikram, K.: *Egypt: Economic Management in a Period of Transition*, John Hopkins University Press, Baltimore, 1980, pp. 343–4.

It is easy to see why Egypt did not feel the need to borrow during those years. There were still some unpaid sterling balances from Britain's war debt as well as an unused sum already paid but not used before the revolution, and hence added to the reserves. Development efforts were still modest throughout the 1950's, the government being more preoccupied with political rather than development issues and still believing in the possibility of relying on private investment, both domestic and foreign, for achieving rapid growth. Public investment did not constitute a big burden on the balance of payments at that time, while potential private investors were waiting to discover the true orientation of the new regime. Total commodity imports therefore increased only very slightly during that period (by 5% between 1952 and 1958) and the deficit on current account in 1957–58 was smaller than it was in 1951–52.[3]

The balance-of-payments picture during the following seven years (1959–65) was radically different. Those were the years of ambitious development targets and comprehensive planning, high investment rates and income redistribution measures. The investment rate rose from 12.5% of GDP in 1959/60 to 17.8% in 1964/65 and there was a notable redistribution in favour of lower-income groups leading to a rise in the rate of increase in private consumption. What may be surprising is not the increase in the pressure on the balance of payments and the emergence of the need for external borrowing, but that the need to borrow was not greater than it actually turned out to be, considering the additional increase in public expenditure on both social services and the army. Thus, after being virtually constant during the first seven years following the revolution, the average annual value of total commodity imports rose from $558 million during 1952–58 to $824 million during 1959–66. In spite of the significant increase in commodity exports, and in the revenues from the Suez Canal after its nationalization, the deficit on current accounts in 1959–66 was three times as much as it was during 1952–58.[4]

It is often said that the burden on the balance of payments would have been significantly greater during the 1960's but for the sterling balances accumulating from the war years. The fact, however, is that at the beginning of 1959 Britain owed Egypt only 90 million sterling

---

[3] Hansen, B. and Marzouk, G.: *Development and Economic Policy in the UAR (Egypt)*, North-Holland, Amsterdam 1965, pp. 174 and 186–7.

[4] Ikram, *op.cit.*, p. 342.

pounds, a small amount considering the figures of commodity imports just mentioned, and the new obligations which Egypt had to meet as a result of the nationalization of the Canal and the building of the High Dam. These obligations included the payment of 67.5 million sterling pounds as compensation for shareholders in the nationalized Suez Canal Company, for British owners of nationalized property and for the Sudan in return for the inundation of land as a result of the High Dam. In addition to this, there were the compensations which Egypt had to pay to the non-British owners of nationalized property, including Greek, Italian, French, Lebanese and Swiss subjects.[5] What remained from the sterling balances at the beginning of the plan years (1959/60–64/65) was in fact less than half the realized investment of the first year of the plan.

It was inevitable that Egypt would turn to external borrowing. El-Gritly estimates the total of what Egypt actually obtained in loans and grants between June 1958 and June 1965 at L.E. 800 million, consisting of L.E. 300 million of U.S. food aid and L.E. 500 million from the Soviet Union, other eastern bloc countries, and some Western countries and international institutions.[6] External borrowing during that period represented 5% of GDP and financed about 30% of the total investment.[7]

Civilian loans during this period were largely used to finance worthwhile productive projects. Soviet aid went to finance industrial projects and the High Dam, while U.S. food aid was "productively"

---

[5] El-Gritly, A.: *The Economic History of the Revolution: 1952–66* (Arabic), Dar Al-Maaref, Cairo, 1974, p. 128.

[6] *ibid.*, p. 139.

[7] In the June 1993 Symposium referred to in the preface to this book, and henceforth referred as the "June Symposium", doubts were expressed about the validity of the allegation made in the text about the sterling balances which were available to Egypt at the beginning of the five-year plan (1960/65) being too modest compared with the plan requirements, and it was stressed by some participants that the 1960's were, on the whole, fortunate in a number of circumstances which made the development task easier and the recourse to external borrowing much less justified. Reference was made to Suez Canal revenues after 1956, as well as to the easy terms of borrowing. It was also pointed out that economic success is usually easier and the burden of development lighter at earlier stages of development than later. With regard to sterling balances, the comparisons made in the text between what was available of these assets in 1959 and the huge obligations which Egypt had to meet at the time, seem to be a sufficient indicator of the relative modesty of these assets. The present author has no inclination to deny, however, that the development task was made much easier before the 1967 war, by several fortunate domestic and international circumstances. In addition to the much easier terms of borrowing in the 1960's (compared with the 1970's and 1980's), which is mentioned in the

used by allowing a big increase in employment in new projects rather than merely allowing an increase in the consumption of those already employed. The transformation of the economic structure during the first half of the 1960's was quite remarkable when compared with what took place over the two decades preceding or those following that period. The share of the manufacturing industry and electricity in GDP rose from 17% in 1958 to 23% in 1965 and has been lower than this ever since. The share of manufacturing in the total labour force did not increase as rapidly but industrial employment increased during that period more rapidly than it ever did since the time of Mohamed Ali. No less important was the fact that the development effort during the first five-year plan period was of the type that would have allowed, in the absence of severe external shocks, the repayment of external debt over a reasonable range of time. This was made possible not only by the uses to which these external loans were put but also by the easy conditions on which they were obtained.

Both the political and economic conditions of foreign assistance were much softer during this cold-war period than in the later period of detente or in the cold war years of the 1980's. It was much more possible for Third World leaders at that time to play one superpower against the other, with minimum concessions to either of them, and hence to extract the maximum possible amount of foreign aid from both of them without succumbing completely to the will of one or the other. Economic conditions were also highly concessionary, with Soviet loans extended for 12 years at an interest rate of 2.5%, and U.S. food aid being repayable in Egyptian currency, at 4% interest over a period of 30 years. What Khalid Ikram refers to when he mentions credits "obtained at exorbitant interest rates"[8] were short-term bank credits which were made necessary by the sudden

text, the Suez Canal revenues, nationalization of other foreign assets as well as the existence of some obviously rewarding areas of investment at that early stage of development, certainly made many things easier before the shock of 1967. There is no benefit to be reaped from portraying the economic policy makers of the 1960's as the embodiment of economic wisdom and those of later years as capable only of committing economic mistakes. This is obviously not true, but the author finds the tendency of much of the current literature which is hostile to public ownership and state control, to do the exact opposite, equally erroneous. Several important economic mistakes have certainly been committed in the 1960's, but it seems to the present author unacceptable to consider these mistakes responsible for much of what the Egyptian economy is suffering from today.

[8] Ikram, *op.cit.*, p. 344.

suspension by the U.S. of its P.L. 480 assistance to Egypt after 1965. This, together with the 1967 war, constituted the unexpected external shocks that turned the earlier loans into such a heavy burden and also made it imperative to contract new ones.

1.2 *The Impact of the 1967 War*

Egypt's economic fortune started to take a sudden turn for the worse in 1965. When the time came for renewing the P.L. 480 food aid agreement with the U.S., the Egyptian government was told that the U.S. was not ready to consider this renewal for the time being because it disapproved of certain foreign policies of the Egyptian government. Only temporary extensions of 3–6 month durations were allowed until American aid was stopped completely in February 1967. This was accompanied by a big decline in total aid extended to Egypt by Western countries and international institutions. The annual average of this aid (including U.S. food aid) declined from $200 million during 1961–66 to only $16 million during 1967–69.

The situation was made much worse by the 1967 war which caused heavy losses in foreign exchange. The Suez Canal, which used to bring to Egypt $164 million annually during the previous seven years, or about 30% more than the annual average of U.S. aid, was closed in 1967. Sinai oil was lost to Egypt, the Suez refineries destroyed and tourism, which brought about $100 million annually before the war, suffered a big decline. One million inhabitants of the Suez Canal towns were forced to migrate and had to be rehoused in other Egyptian cities at great cost.

Aid from the Soviet bloc did increase after 1967 but was far from being sufficient to compensate for the loss of Western aid. Annual average disbursements from the Soviet bloc during 1967–72 was about $140 million compared with $116 million during the ten years (1954–64)[9] and with the decline in Western aid by $184 million already referred to. The main source of external aid to Egypt in the years following 1967 was the Khartoum Agreement of 1968 signed by Saudi Arabia, Kuwait and Libya and according to which Egypt obtained grants amounting on average to $286 million annually. This was a significant amount, being not much less than the annual average of

[9] Amin, G.: *The Modernization of Poverty*, Brill, Leiden, 1974, p. 9.

the total assistance obtained by Egypt from both East and West before 1967. But Egypt still had to find by itself the way to meet almost all the economic consequences of the 1967 war. These included on top of the losses just mentioned, the burden of increased military expenses, aiming at the liberation of Sinai. Added to all this was the fact that installments of some loans contracted before 1967 had now to be repaid. These installments amounted to about $240 million annually during the period 1967–72.[10] It appears therefore that Egypt after 1967 was not only facing extremely arduous economic and political conditions but was also obliged to pay the price of the ambitious development effort of the pre-1967 years.

There were apparently three options facing the political leadership in Egypt following the 1967 war. One was to forgo military expenditure, accept the conditions offered for peace, however humiliating they may be (if indeed such an offer was at all made), for the sake of continued economic development; another was to press for even lower consumption levels to compensate for the decline in resources and maintain both the military and development efforts, and a third option was to forgo rapid development while allowing some minimal increase in consumption in order to finance the preparation for another war. There did not seem to be a fourth option since there were not enough external sources of revenue sufficient to finance the same level of investment as prevailed in 1960–65, as well as an increased military expenditure. The first two options were rejected for political reasons. With the political leadership so much weakened by the defeat of 1967, it became very reluctant to antagonize important sections of the population by any harsh measures aiming at raising the rate of saving. The humiliation of the defeat was apparently enough, while to accept an equally humiliating peace was beyond the capacity of both the political leadership and most of the population. Economic development had therefore to pay the full price of the 1967 war.

For about eight years (1967–75) Egypt witnessed one of the bleakest periods in its modern economic history. Investment declined from 17.2% of GDP in 1964–65 to 13% during 1967–75. Private consumption remained virtually constant (65%) while public consumption increased significantly to allow for greater military expenditure. But even with this big reduction in investment, the balance of pay-

---

[10] Ikram, *op.cit.*, p. 344.

ments continued to deteriorate. The deficit on current account increased by 86% (from $202 million in 59–66 to $375 million in 67–72). This, together with debt service obligations, forced Egypt to make heavy use of Western suppliers' credit as well as short-term credit from commercial banks.

It is important, however, to note certain differences between the development of external debt in the last three years of Nasser's regime (1967–70) and the first five years of Sadat's (1970–75). The earlier period relied much more on grants (mainly according to the Khartoum Agreement) than on suppliers' credit and short-term borrowing, the last two sources of finance not exceeding 27% of the total foreign exchange deficit. On Nasser's death in 1970, Egypt's total public civilian external debt (long and medium-term) had reached $1.7 billion. No exact figures are available for military debt, short-term public civilian or private sector debt at that time, but there are estimates of suppliers' credit of about $133 million, of short-term bank credit of about $37 million and of military debt of about $3 billion. Total Egyptian external debt of all kinds (including public and private, civilian and military, long, medium and short-term) was therefore in the neighbourhood of $5 billion in 1970. For 1975, there is no reliable figure for military debt but civilian external public debt (including short-term public debt) had now reached $6.3 billion compared with about $1.8 billion in 1970. The seeds for the rapid growth of external debt were therefore sown between 1970 and 1975. Public civilian debt grew by 350% during those five years. Compared with an average annual rate of growth of 9% in long and medium-term external public civilian debt during the 1960's, its growth rate was 23% during the period 1970–75. Short-term external debt grew at 25% annually in the 1960's and 55% during 1970–75.[11]

The relatively rapid growth of external civilian debt during the first half of the 1970's when compared with the three years following the 1967 war, was mainly due to the rapid growth of imports. Exports of goods and services did increase rapidly during 1970–75 (by 240% in 5 years) but imports increased much more rapidly (by 350%).[12] This is to be compared with the previous 5 years (1964/5–1969/70) during which the value of exports of goods and services

[11] These figures and estimates of various types of debt are taken or calculated from: Ikram, *op.cit.*, pp. 343–4 and 362–5, IMF: *ARE: Recent Economic Developments*, June 19, 1984 (mimeo.), p. 66, and World Bank: *World Debt Tables*, 1985.

[12] *World Debt Tables*, 1985.

declined by 7%, for the reasons referred to above and largely associated with the 1967 war, but imports *decreased* by even more (15%) as a result of government policy of reducing investment.[13]

This development of exports and imports during 1970–75 must be partly blamed on the deterioration in Egypt's terms of trade with regard to Egypt's main export item at the time (cotton) and its main imported good (wheat). While the international price of a ton of wheat rose 4.5 times during 1970–75 (from L.E. 25 to L.E. 112), that of cotton increased only about 100% (from L.E. 530 to L.E. 1068). As a result, a ton of cotton brought to Egypt in 1975 less than half the amount of wheat it brought in 1970.[14] But even this higher import burden cannot be wholly blamed on external conditions for one must raise the question why domestic production failed so badly in meeting domestic requirements. Per capita output of grains was in fact 5% lower in 1974/5 than it was in 1970/1, and per capita consumption 9% higher. This is not mainly the fault of the 1970's, since much of this failure must be due to lower investment in agriculture in earlier years, partly due again to the impact of the 1967 war.

The main blame that could be addressed to the economic policies of the early 1970's seems to go to two main errors: one is the sudden introduction of a much more liberal trade system, allowing a rapid increase in imports of a great variety of goods, at a time of severe foreign exchange shortage. This liberalization of imports is sometimes excused by reference to the great need of many productive activities at the time for imported intermediate goods and spare parts after a long period of scarcity, import licensing and underutilization of industrial capacity. The need of repairing the infrastructure which had greatly deteriorated since 1967, is also sometimes mentioned as necessitating a big increase in imports. While it is true that following the 1973 war, imports of capital and intermediate goods did increase rapidly (threefold and fivefold respectively between 1973 and 1975), imports of other much less necessary goods also increased rapidly (including imports of private motorcars which increased more than fourfold during those two years, and imports of nondurable consumer goods which increased more than fivefold), so that their value in 1975 was not much less than the total imports of

---

[13] See on the impact of this policy on imports: Mabro, R.: *The Egyptian Economy, 1952–72*, Clarendon Press, Oxford, 1974, p. 177.

[14] Ikram, *op.cit.*, p. 224.

capital goods.[15] "Capital and intermediate goods" imported into Egypt include, in any case, such things as trucks, building materials and spare parts for motor cars, which largely serve consumption rather than production activities. Thus, while the first half of the 1970's witnessed a great housing boom, several industries recorded an absolute decline in total output, including cement, paper, sugar, cigarettes, tyres and buses.[16] As for public utilities, their share in the total investment of the period (1972–75) did not in fact exceed 4%,[17] and most of what was spent on them after the 1973 war consisted of the reconstruction of Suez Canal towns which were justified with reference more to political considerations than to development requirements, and much of it was closer to consumption than to production needs.

(ii) The other error of economic policy was the use of very costly short-term credit to finance much of this increase in imports. Short-term debt to commercial banks at interest rates sometimes exceeding 15%, together with suppliers' credit, constituted as much as 35% of the total civilian debt of Egypt in 1975. Total short-term debt of Egypt multiplied about seven times between 1970 and 1975 (from $170 million to $1168 million).[18] The burden on the balance of payments created by this kind of loans consisted not only of high interest payments but also of the accumulation of charges resulting from failure to pay on time.[19]

1.3 *Borrowing during Years of Prosperity*

The mid 1970's marks another turning point in Egypt's recent economic history, but in contrast to that of the mid 1960's, this time it was for the better. In 1975, the debt situation seems to have reached a very low ebb, which Sadat used a strange but expressive term to describe, namely, "a zero situation", and excused himself by offering

[15] National Bank of Egypt: *Economic Bulletin*, 1985, no. 1, and also Ramzy Zaki: *Studies in Egypt's External Debt*, (Arabic), Madbouli Bookshop, Cairo, 1985, p. 385.

[16] IBRD: *ARE: Economic Prospects and External Capital Requirements, March 22, 1977*, (mimeo.), Statistical Appendix.

[17] Ikram, *op.cit.*, p. 405.

[18] Ikram, *op.cit.*, p. 362.

[19] Some participants in the June symposium denied that civilian loans during the 1960's were largely used to finance "productive" projects. They may have been directed to productive "sectors", but they were often "unproductively" used. What is meant is presumably that the allocation of investment in the 1960's was often

even stranger reasons, one being that nobody had actually informed him of how serious the situation had become, and another was that he thought the figures of external debt presented to him were in dollars while in fact they were in sterling pounds.[20] In 1975, about one-third of all of Egypt's external debt was due for repayment during

---

objectionable and the implementation and management of projects inefficient. It was also pointed out that the impact of these investments on the balance of payments was on the whole negative, since what was meant to be an import-substitution strategy ended by being a "substitution of imports by imports". It was also denied that investments in the 1960's were of the type that could have allowed the servicing of the loans over a reasonable period of time had the 1967 war, with all its negative impact on the balance of payments, not occurred. The High Dam was the example given for these investments. It was also argued that the maintenance of infrastructure in the 1960's was so badly neglected that a heavy burden was to be carried by later periods.

Even if allowance is made of all these objections, the allegation in the text may continue to hold, namely, that the economic policies of the 1960's are less to blame for the serious debt situation which became obvious since the mid 1970's, than the repercussions of the 1967 war and the two policies of import liberalization and excessive short-term borrowing since the early 1970's. But the present author also holds that the misallocation of investment and inefficient economic management before 1967 are highly exaggerated in the more recent literature, as compared with the earlier assessments made by less biased observers of Egypt's economic policy in the 1960's and of its first five-year plan. (See for instance Hansen, B. and Marzouk, G.: *Development and Economic Policy in the UAR* (*Egypt*), North-Holland, Amsterdam, 1965 and Mabro, R.: *The Egyptian Economy, 1952–72*, Clarendon Press, Oxford, 1974.)

The impact of the investment policy of the 1960's on the balance of payments, with regard to both agricultural and manufactured exports, is shown in Chapters 4 and 5 of this book to be much more positive than the critics allege. The contribution of the High Dam in reducing Egypt's import requirements may have taken a long time to materialize, but one is at a loss to find a comparable investment project in the 1970's or the 1980's as far as its contribution to the reduction of Egypt's import requirements. No cost-benefit analysis of the High Dam has yet been made to show the contribution of the Dam in saving Egypt's agricultural output from the serious droughts of the late 1980's.

The allegation that much of the growth of Egypt's indebtedness in the 1970's and 1980's is due to the neglect of maintenance of infrastructure in the 1960's, has grown to become something of a myth. In the text, I have shown how little the 1970's have contributed to infrastructure development, but the "neglect" of infrastructure in the 1960's is also highly exaggerated. According to Bent Hansen's assessment of the first five-year plan (1960–65), investment in "public utilities and other services including government", constituted as much as 10.1% of total actual investments during the plan years (see his article: "Planning and Economic Growth in the U.A.R: 1960–65", in Vatikiotis, P. (ed.): *Egypt since the Revolution*, Allen and Unwin, London, 1968, p. 35) This is a much higher share than in the first half of the 1970's (less than 4%, see Ikram, K.: *Egypt: Economic Management in a Period of Transition*, Johns Hopkins University Press, Baltimore, 1980, p. 405), about equal to its share in 1977–1981/2 (10.6%, see IMF: A.R.E., *Recent Economic Developments*, June 19, 1984, *mimeo*, p. 4).

[20] Quoted in Hussein, A.: *The Egyptian Economy from Independence to Dependence 1974–79* (in Arabic), Dar El Wahda, Beirut, 1981, vol. 2, pp. 142–3.

the following two years and in 1975 alone, Egypt was obliged to pay $2084 million in servicing these short-term debts, an amount equal to 78% of Egypt's proceeds of all exports in that year.[21]

Only two years later, the situation became radically different and it looked as if a whole decade of accumulating difficulties was coming to an end. The last four years of Sadat's reign (1977–81) were almost unprecedented in Egypt's modern history, in terms of growth of income and foreign exchange revenues. During those four years, the rate of growth of GDP reached 8–9% in real terms, oil exports, which did not bring more than $162 million in 1977, multiplied almost ten times to $1.5 billion in 1981 as a result of the rise in both oil prices and output, while invisible exports, mainly labour remittances, increased from $998 million to $4 billion during the same period. Egypt's terms of trade rose by 81% in those four years and its total foreign exchange revenues multiplied about four times.[22]

Those conditions were obviously favourable for an attempt not only to stop the trend of increasing indebtedness but to bring about a significant reduction in it. The value of the increase in total exports of goods and services between 1977 and 1981 was about $7 billion, which constitutes 86% of the total external civilian long and medium-term debts in 1977. What happened, however, was that these debts, which amounted to $4.8 billion in 1975 and $8.1 billion in 1977, increased during the next four years by no less than 76% to reach $14.3 billion in 1981.

The explanation is, of course, that imports were allowed to increase faster than exports, however rapidly these may have been rising, so that the deficit on current account more than doubled in those four years. It is not true that the importation of luxury goods carries most of the blame, as is often said or implied, for about 60% of the increase in commodity imports during that period consisted of capital and intermediate goods and 18% was due to the increase in imports of wheat, maize and flour.[23] This rapid increase in imports of capital and intermediate goods was a reflection of a striking rise in the rate of investment to about 30% of GDP. What was blameworthy is that the greatest part of the new investments was not of the

---

[21] Zaki, R.: "The External Debt issue" in Abdel-Khalek, G. (ed.): *The Open Door Policy: Its Roots, Harvest and Future* (Arabic), Arab Center for Research and Publishing, Cairo, 1982, pp. 193–4.

[22] National Bank of Egypt: *Economic Bulletin*, 1985, No. 1, p. 105.

[23] *ibid.*

type that should have been financed by external borrowing and least of all, at commercial rates of interest. Most of the investment went to trade, housing and infrastructure so that the highest rates of growth of output between 1977 and 1981/2, outside oil and the Suez Canal, were not in industry or agriculture but in trade and finance (12.5% annually), construction (11.3%), government services including infrastructure (10.6%) and transport, communications and storage (8.3%).[24]

Another important source of blame for the rapid growth in external debt between 1977 and 1981 was the rapid increase in military expenditure, even though those were the years of "peace", starting with Sadat's surprise visit to Jerusalem in November 1977, and including the Camp David agreement of 1978 and the peace treaty of 1979. Arms purchases during those years were financed mainly by external borrowing at the very high commercial interest rates prevailing at the time. An 1984 IMF report mentions that military expenditure in Egypt increased at an annual rate of 20% in the years following 1979, reaching 32% in the last year of Sadat's rule (1981).[25]

1.4 *External Debt during Mubarak's First Five-Year Plan*

Sadat's two main economic legacies to President Mubarak were a much bigger external debt and a more distorted economic structure than Sadat had received from his predecessor.

Between Nasser's death in 1970 and the assassination of Sadat in 1981, total external civilian public debt, both long and medium-term but not including short-term debt, increased from $1.7 billion to $14.3 billion, more than an eightfold increase. Other kinds of external debt (short-term and military debts) increased from about $3 billion to $15 billion, so that total Egyptian external indebtedness of all kinds, civilian and military, public and private, long, medium and short-term, multiplied six times in a decade, from about $5 billion in 1970 to about $30 billion in 1981. These last two amounts of debt represented respectively 43% of GDP in 1970 and 141% of GDP in 1981. To service civilian debt alone, Egypt had to pay in 1981 no less than $2.9 billion ($1.3 in repayment of principal and $1.6 in interest

---

[24] IMF: *Arab Republic of Egypt: Recent Economic Developments*, June 19, 1984, (mimeo.) p. 4.

[25] *ibid.*, p. 38.

payments). The ratio of debt service to all proceeds of foreign exchange was 28% in 1981, about the same as it was in 1970,[26] but with the important difference that the total value of exports of goods and services in 1981 was more than ten times its level in 1970.

Economic structure had continued to deteriorate since the mid 1960's, with the continuous increase in the share of services (as well as oil after 1975) at the expense of the commodity sectors, so that by the end of the 1970's, Egypt was less of an industrial nation than it was in 1965.

With the change in the political leadership in 1981 the need was expressed for a serious reconsideration of economic policies with the aim of arresting the deterioration both in the external debt situation and in economic structure. One view which was forcefully expressed in the February 1982 economic conference called by President Mubarak to discuss alternative solutions to the economic crisis, and repeatedly expressed in the annual conferences of Egyptian economists since 1976, was to introduce severe restrictions on imports, including some capital and intermediate goods, even at the price of a reduction in the rates of investment and growth of output, as well as a big reduction in military expenditure. The reduction in investment was to be compensated for by the rationalization of investment allocation and by income redistribution measures. But the policies actually adopted after 1981 were in fact basically a continuation of the policies of the 1970's: high levels of investment with only mildly greater restrictions on imports, heavy military expenditure and continuing reliance on external borrowing.

In fact, what was called the first five-year plan for the years 1982/3–1986/7, did not seem to give high priority to the reduction of external debt, even though "self reliance" was one of its declared aims. Civilian external indebtedness was planned to increase by about 25% during the five years of the plan, in order to achieve a rate of investment of 25% of GDP and a rate of growth of output of 8.1%. As soon as the plan was launched, however, it became clear that even if the high level of indebtedness was not sufficient reason for more modest investment goals, the change in external circumstances

---

[26] IMF: *ARE: Recent Economic Developments*, June 19, 1984, (mimeo.) p. 66; Zaki, R.: *Studies in Egypt's External Debt* (Arabic), Madbouli Bookshop, 1985, p. 407; *Middle East Economic Survey*, March 30, 1987 and Butter D.: "Debt and Egypt's Financial Policies" in Tripp, Charles and Owen, R. (eds.): *Egypt Under Mubarak*, Routledge, London, 1989, pp. 123–136.

should have justified greater restraint all around. For during the first four years of the 1980's, oil revenues declined by 36%, and the other three main sources of foreign exchange (labour remittances, Suez Canal and tourism) which are influenced in various degrees by the oil market, were virtually stagnant. The flow of private foreign investment remained constant at about one billion dollars a year, while exports of primary commodities, other than oil, did not increase by more than 4% annually. With only a modest increase in exports of manufactures, the total value of exports of goods and services in 1985/86 was actually lower than in 1981/82 by 11%. Meanwhile, Egypt had to continue to pay increasing amounts of interest on previous debts. Some new restrictions on imports were introduced but they were far from sufficient to arrest the deterioration in the balance of current account where the deficit rose from $1.7 billion in 1981/82 to $3.5 billion in 1985/6.

On June 30, 1986, Egypt's total indebtedness was 26% greater than in 1981, rising from $30 billion to $37.8 billion in those five years, and civilian external debt of all kinds increased by 16%. These are much lower rates of increase than those of the last five years of Sadat, when total external indebtedness increased about threefold. This is all the more remarkable when one notes that external conditions, largely connected with oil prices, were much more fortunate in the earlier period and hence the need to borrow much less.

It should also be noted that a significant proportion of the debt disbursed during the 1980's had in fact been contracted during the 1970's. This proportion was estimated by the Minister of Planning at two-thirds of the increase in external civilian debt between 1981 and 1986.[27] The need for the rehabilitation of infrastructure could also be more justly used as a justification for the growth of debt in the 1980's than in earlier years, since the notable improvement in infrastructure, particularly in transport and communications, water and sewage works, was due more to external debts disbursed during the 1980's than before.

One can, however, address two criticisms which were mentioned earlier in connection with Sadat's economic policy, and are just as applicable to the first five years of Mubarak. One relates to the financing of infrastructure projects which yield no direct income, by funds borrowed at high interest rates. External debt was therefore

[27] An interview with the Minister of Planning, *Al-Musawwar* (a Cairo Arabic Weekly), July 3, 1987, p. 22.

growing at a much faster rate than the ability of the economy to service it. The other criticism relates to the continued growth of military debt. Military debt which ironically started to increase rapidly after the 1979 peace treaty, increased again by about 80% in five years (1981–86). Starting from 1985, military aid from the U.S. took the form of grants, but what had already been borrowed to finance military purchases continued to burden the balance of payments with interest rates of 12% on average. Failure to service this military debt was also punishable by increasing interest rates by four percentage points (to 16%) on any delay of 60 days or more. This started to occur quite frequently from 1984 onward so that in 1985, no more than 38% of what should have been paid in servicing this debt was actually paid.

By 1986, the debt situation was therefore considerably worse than it was at the beginning of the decade, even though the growth of debt was slower than in the 1970's. The structure of the debt also showed a much greater imbalance than in 1970. While in 1970, the shares of East and West in Egypt's total civilian debt were almost equal (43% and 46% respectively), the share of the latter rose to 68% in 1986 (25% to the U.S., 33.3% to other Western countries, Japan and Australia and 9.5% to the World Bank group and IMF) while the share of the Eastern bloc declined to 3% (see Table 1.1). In the light of all this, Egypt seemed very ill-prepared in 1986 to receive a new external shock. But this was unfortunately what happened.

TABLE 1.1
Percentage Distribution of Egypt's Public Sector External Debt at the End of June 1986

Creditor	%	Creditor	%
U.S.A.	25.0	IMF	1.1
W. Europe, Japan & Canada	30.0	Comecon Countries & China	3.1
Arab & Islamic Countries	11.8	Australia & Other Countries	2.8
Arab Aid Agencies	8.9	Regional Institutions(1)	1.0
World Bank	5.0	Locally Incorporated Banks	4.1
IDA	3.3	Other	3.9
		Total	100.0

(1) Includes African Development Bank, European Investment Bank and Islamic Development Bank.

Source: Calculated from Butter, D.: "Debt and Egypt's Financial Policies", in Tripp, Charles and Owen, R.: *Egypt Under Mubarak, Routledge*, London, 1989, p. 125.

Ext. shock in -86

1.5 *The Reckoning*

A serious external shock hit the Egyptian economy early in 1986 in the form of a sharp fall in oil prices. This did not only affect Egypt's own oil revenues but hit Egypt indirectly as well, by the levelling off of labour remittances from the oil-rich countries and the decline in Arab tourism in Egypt. Rates of growth of output which had shown regular decline since the early 1980's, showed a sharp decline after 1986. After reaching 8% in real terms between 1975 and 1982, the annual growth rate in GNP declined to 5% in the following three years (1983–5), and then to about 1% between 1985/86 and 1989/90. With a population growth of about 2.7%, the standard of living must have fallen during the second half of the 1980's at an annual rate of about 1.7% a year.

The situation was aggravated by the fact that this fall in oil revenues coincided with a steep rise in Egypt's debt service obligations. According to an IMF source,[28] these obligations in 1985/86 were no less than $5.5 billion ($2.9 billion for repayment of principal and $2.6 billion in interest payment), which was almost double the debt service of 1981, and constituted more than 50% of the value of all exports and services in 1985/86. Debt service obligations in that year, if they were to be actually paid, would have taken all the income from oil, the Suez Canal and tourism, in addition to about a third of labour remittances.

But Egypt was, of course, unable to meet these obligations and had in fact already been accumulating arrears in servicing its debts for some years. As early as 1979, Egypt had declared that it was not going to meet its debt obligations towards the Arab countries which condemned the Camp David agreement that year. This decision was directed to debts of about $4 billion and since then, Egypt stopped meeting its obligations to other Arab countries including those owed to the "Gulf Organization for the Development of Egypt" established in 1976. In 1980, Egypt stopped servicing its military debts to the Soviet Union, also following Soviet condemnation of the Camp David agreement, and was soon after to cease servicing its debt to Iran.

[28] Hasan, P.: "Structural Adjustment in Selected Arab Countries", paper presented to the symposium entitled *Adjustment Policies and Development Strategies in the Arab World*, organized by IMF and the Arab Monetary Fund in Abu Dhabi, 16–18 February 1987.

Delay in meeting debt obligations to some Western countries had already started, so that total arrears were estimated in 1985/86 at about $2 billion.[29]

It was inevitable that Egypt's external debt would grow more rapidly after 1986 compared with the previous five years, though the rate of growth of debt never approached that of the 1970's. Table 1.2 shows the growth and structure of external debt in those years and indicates an increase in total debt by 21% in the three years following the shock of 1986, reaching $45.7 in June 1989. Actual interest payments ate up more than 50% of all the proceeds from commodity exports. The three main sources of foreign exchange other than oil, namely, workers' remittances, the Suez Canal and tourism, brought together in 1989/90 about twice the proceeds of all commodity exports (see Table 3.1) but even with this, Egypt was still left with a deficit on current account, not including official transfers, of $2294 million, i.e. over one-fifth of all commodity imports. Official transfers in that year reduced the deficit on current account by about 50%, but this left Egypt with a deficit of $1214 million even though it was at the same time failing to pay more than one-third of its interest obligations (see Table 1.3).

The situation on the eve of the Gulf crisis which erupted in August 1990 was therefore quite grim. By that time, total external debt had increased to $47.6 billion, or more than 150% of GDP, making Egypt's external debt burden one of the highest in the world, and higher, in relative terms, than the deservedly-famous Egyptian debt of a little over a century ago (about 100% of GDP) which led to the dethronement of Egypt's Khedive Ismail and to its occupation by Britain. In 1990, the debt service obligations had risen to $6 billion (54% of the total value of all exports of goods and services), commercial and official sources of external credit were tightening and the government was facing difficulties in financing vital food imports.

1.6 *Relief at a price*

The Gulf crisis of 1990/91 was associated with a number of largely unexpected developments including its impact on external debt.

[29] U.S. Embassy in Cairo: *Report on the Egyptian Economy*, December 1986, p. 25.

TABLE 1.2
External Debt Outstanding

($million at end of period)

	83/84	84/85	85/86	86/87	87/88	88/89
Supplier's Credit	4260	4650	5562	6160	7518	8509
IBRD and IDA	1554	1752	1903	1963	2011	n/a
GODE*	2269	2381	2406	2449	2529	n/a
Other Multilateral Loans	413	428	603	682	685	n/a
Bilateral Civilian Loans	9740	10365	10759	12012	12756	24817(a)
Military Loans	7330	9380	8936	9447	10495	
Total Medium and Long-term Public and Public Guaranteed Debt	25566	28956	30169	332713	35994	38591
Short-term Debt	5655	5637	4929	4388	4321	4344
Private Sector Debt	1849	1807	2750	2750	2826	2818
Total Debt	33070	36400	37848	39851	43141	45753

(*) The Gulf Organization for the Development of Egypt.
(a) Includes also military loans.

Source: IMF: Report on Recent Economic Developments in Egypt, January 1990.

TABLE 1.3
Interest Payments Compared with Interest Obligations (U.S. million)

	1985/86	1986/7	1987/8	1988/9
Interest Payments	1422	1093	785	1016
Interest Obligations	2443	2385	2866	3423

Sources: as for Table 1.2.

Commitments of financial and commodity assistance to Egypt, in response to the Gulf crisis and to the Egyptian government's estimate of expected losses, started to be provided to Egypt on an impressive scale. Six months after the eruption of the crisis, Egypt obtained commitments of financial assistance (excluding that of the U.S.) amounting to as much as $4726 million, mainly from Saudi Arabia, Kuwait, U.A.E., Germany and Japan (see Table 1.4). Although this sum fell short of the Egyptian government's estimate of the impact of the crisis on the balance of payments ($5900 million) made in the early days of the crisis, and the rate of disbursement was significantly lower than commitments, it nevertheless made a considerable contribution to the balance of payments, so that contrary to all expectations, the year 1990/91 turned out to be a much better year for the balance of payments than any of the previous five years. In addition to $2.4 billion (disbursed) of financial assistance, several western countries provided commodity assistance in the form of grants, with France sending wheat, flour and meat, Canada sending coal and newsprint and Australia diverting a big commercial shipment of wheat, which was on its way to Iraq, to be given as a grant to Egypt.

The United States continued its massive economic aid program to Egypt during 1990/91, at the usual rate of about one billion dollars (disbursements) a year,[30] in addition to a small emergency aid in the form of wheat and flour. But the most important financial contribution by the U.S. to Egypt in response to the crisis, has been the approval by the U.S. administration of the cancellation of 90% of Egypt's military debt to the U.S., reducing this debt by $7.1 billion. This was soon followed by a reduction by some Arab Gulf states of another $6.6 billion of Egypt's debt to them. The two exemptions were expected to reduce Egypt's interest obligations by about one billion dollars annually. Shortly afterwards, negotiations with countries forming the Paris Club led to an agreement in May 1991 whereby Egypt would be exempted from 50% of part of its external debt amounting to $20.2 billion, in three steps: one, constituting an exemption of 15%, was to take place immediately, another exemption of 15% was to take place after 18 months (November 1992) and the last (20%) after another 18 months (May 1994).

Thus, Egypt was to be relieved in May 1991 of $3 billion, to be added to the earlier reductions by the U.S. and some Gulf countries of $13.7 billion; of another $3 billion in November 1992, and of a final $4 billion in May 1994. The last two reductions, however, were tied to Egypt's performance in the implementation of the IMF and

---

[30] Since U.S. economic assistance to Egypt was resumed in 1975, it has been the most important single source of foreign aid to Egypt. Total U.S. economic assistance between 1975 and 1990 totaled about $16 billion, of which $6.7 billion (42%) was in the form of project financing, $4.6 billion (28%) according to U.S. Commodity Import Program, $3.5 billion (22%) in the form of agricultural aid according to P.L. 480, and $1.3 billion (8%) in cash transfers. All these figures refer to actual disbursements and not merely to commitments.

TABLE 1.4
Financial Assistance to Egypt
in Response to the Gulf Crisis
(up to 31 January 1991)

(US $million)

Donor	Commitments	Disbursements	Donor	Commitments	Disbursements
Europe:			*Arab Countries:*		
EC Budget	254	16	Kuwait	1015	555
Belgium	16	6	S. Arabia	1688	1208
France	50	0	U.A.E.	420	420
Germany	673	154	*Other Countries:*		
Ireland	6	0	Australia	1	0
Italy	75	0	Canada	22	0
Luxembourg	1	0	Korea	23	0
Netherlands	18	18	Japan	440	0
Norway	2	2			
Spain	12	0	Total	4726	2379
Sweden	10	0			

Source: Ministry of International Cooperation.

World Bank recommendations for economic reform.

Egypt's external debt was therefore reduced from $47.6 billion in June 1990 to about $34 billion by February 1991, as a result of the cancellation of $7.1 billion by the U.S. and $6.6 billion by the Gulf countries. In July 1991, it was further reduced to $31 billion, and if the other 35% reduction agreed upon in the Paris Club was to take place, and assuming that no addition to the external debt is to occur up to mid 1994, Egypt's external debt at that time would fall to about $24 billion, a decline of 50% from its level in mid 1990.

In addition to all this, and as a result of the completion of the agreement with the IMF in April 1991 which made the Paris Club agreement possible, new IMF and World Bank loans were extended to Egypt, including interest-free loans from the International Development Association.[31]

The second exemption which was due in November 1992 was delayed but finally approved, while the third exemption, due in mid

[31] Over the years, Egypt has obtained about one billion dollars in soft loans from IDA, but was deprived of the right to borrow in 1981 as a result of the rise in per capita income in the late 1970's. Egypt was readmitted to borrow from IDA in October 1990.

1994, was again delayed owing to the disagreement between Egypt and the IMF over the speed of implementation of economic measures urged by the IMF and the World Bank. Since 1987, and particularly after the Paris Club meeting of May 1991, Egypt has gone a long way in meeting the demands of IMF and the World bank for the implementation of the program of stabilization, structural adjustment and economic liberalization, including the promulgation of a new public sector company law in 1991, allowing the establishment of holding companies which would in their turn provide a legal basis for privatization. But since then, the actual process of privatization has been slow and it has been reported that this constitutes the main subject of complaint from the two international organizations and the main obstruction to the final reduction in external debt.

Meanwhile, the government has prepared another five-year plan (usually referred to as the "third" plan) to cover the period 1992/3–1996/7, in which reliance on external sources would be reduced to 14% of the financial requirements of the plan (L.E. 20.6 billion out of L.E. 145.1 billion). Of the foreign capital required, excluding private foreign investment, 30% would be in the form of grants, 62% in loans and 8% in the form of other credit facilities.[32] This is a much more ambitious target, as far as mobilization of domestic capital is concerned, than was ever envisaged in Egypt in its planning history, including Nasser's five-year plan of 1959/60–1964/65. This optimism is based on the expected results of the structural adjustment and liberalization programs. The impact of these programs on the rates of domestic saving and investment, on the growth of the commodity sectors as compared with services, as well as on agricultural and manufactured exports, is expected to eliminate the need for foreign sources to finance consumption needs, and to confine the need for such sources to those projects where the expected return on investment exceeds the cost of borrowing. One major aim of the following chapters is to assess the realism of such hopes.

---

[32] Ministry of Planning: *Preliminary Framework of the Third Five-Year Plan (1992/3–1996/7)*, (in Arabic), Volume I, p. 180.

CHAPTER TWO

SAVINGS AND INVESTMENT

2.1 *Saving and investment rates*

Egypt's problem of increasing foreign indebtedness could be seen as mainly the result of its failure to mobilize enough savings. This failure to raise the rate of saving has in fact been one of the gloomiest features of Egypt's economic performance since the first five-year plan of 1959/60–1964/65,[1] but it has been particularly striking since the mid 1980's. Table 2.1 shows that over the last quarter of a century, foreign sources of capital were relied upon to cover no less than a quarter of total investment, but after 1985, foreign capital financed as much as one-half of investment, bringing the country to a worse situation than that which prevailed before the rise in oil prices in

TABLE 2.1
National Savings, Investment and Net Inflow of Foreign Resources
(as Percentages of GNP at Current Market Prices)

Period	Gross Saving	Gross Investment	Net Inflow of Foreign Resources
1953/54 to 1955/56	13.0	14.7	1.7
1956/57 to 1957/58	10.8	13.6	2.8
1958/59 to 1959/60	11.5	13.5	2.0
1960/61 to 1964/65	12.7	17.4	4.7
1965/66 to 1966/67	13.7	16.6	2.9
1967/68 to 1970/71	9.3	13.2	3.9
1971/72 to 1973	6.3	13.0	6.7
1974 to 1978	18.1	27.5	9.4
1979 to 1983/84	17.1	29.4	12.3
1985 to 1989	10.8	21.6	10.8

Sources: Hansen, B.: *The Political Economy of Poverty, Equity and Growth: Egypt and Turkey*, A World Bank Comparative Study, Oxford University Press, Oxford, 1991, p. 192, except for 1985–89, from World Bank: *Trends in Developing Economies: 1990*, Washington D.C., 1990, p. 178.

[1] Such was Bent Hansen's judgement of the results of this early plan, see his paper "Planning and Economic Growth in the U.A.R.: 1960–65", in Vatikiotis, P. (ed.): *Egypt Since the Revolution*, Allen & Unwin, London, 1968.

1973. The rate of saving in 1988 and 1989 was as low as 6.8% and 5.7% of GNP, constituting no more than 36% and 30% of total investment respectively.[2]

A complete explanation of the persistence of low saving rates in Egypt could invoke virtually all of Egypt's economic ills, but different writers tend to emphasize different factors. While the reports of international organizations tend to emphasize the wastes of government consumption and the inefficiency of public enterprises resulting in low profits and low savings, Egyptian officials' statements tend to emphasize rapid population growth. Among the factors responsible for the rapid growth of public consumption, two factors tend to receive the greatest emphasis: the subsidy system, and the rapid growth of government employment. The inefficiency of public enterprises is attributed mainly to excessive bureaucratic control and centralization, administrative fixing of prices and weak incentives. But there are many other factors that could be at least as important in explaining the low rate of saving which get much less emphasis.

To begin with, government consumption does not appear to be, at least since the early 1980's, the main culprit behind the decline in the rate of saving. In fact, since 1985, government consumption has shown virtually no growth at all in real terms, while private consumption continued to grow rapidly so that, while the share of government consumption in GDP declined, the share of private consumption rose significantly from 67% in 1982 to 80.1% in 1989 (see Table 2.2). The government appears to have shown considerably greater restraint than the public in the face of the declining rate of growth of income.

TABLE 2.2
Share of Private and Public Consumption in GDP
(at current market prices)

	1982	83	84	85	86	87	88	89
Public Consumption	17.8	17.2	18.0	17.2	16.5	14.5	14.2	14.2
Private Consumption	67.0	65.0	64.6	66.3	68.9	78.6	78.9	80.1

Sources: World Bank: *Arab Republic of Egypt: Economic Readjustment with Growth*, 1990, vol. 2, p. 6; and World World Bank: *Trends in Developing Economies: 1990*, p. 178.

[2] World Bank: *Trends in Developing Economies*, 1990, p. 178.

Professor Bent Hansen, examining the trend of both parts of consumption since the late 1950's, points at the interesting fact that the growth rate of government consumption has actually been declining steadily since the 1960's from 12% in 1960–65 to 4.2% in 1973–1981/82, and we have just seen that this trend continued through the 1980's. The growth rate of private consumption has, on the contrary, been rising from 5.1% in 1960–65 to 8.6% in 1974–1981/2[3] after a slight decline in the intervening period, and became even higher than the rate of growth of GDP at current prices after 1985.

2.2 *Public Consumption*

In examining the factors behind the growth of public consumption one cannot help noting the little attention usually given to expenditure on armaments. Professor Hansen does note that the relatively high rate of growth of government consumption in the 1960's (12%) and its decline afterwards had a great deal to do with conditions of war and peace,[4] but it may be remarked that variations in expenditure on armaments in the case of Egypt at least, seem to have been determined mainly by factors other than whether there was peace or war. We have already seen in chapter I, that military expenditure continued at a high pace well after the 1973 war. Immediately after the peace treaty of 1979, Egypt contracted a big military loan with the U.S. and military expenditure continued to grow for at least another decade. The items of government expenditure that appear from table 2.3 to have risen most sharply during the 1980's are however, neither military expenditure nor governemnt subsidies but rather expenditure on investment, wages and salaries and, most rapidly of all, interest on government debt.

While the government has been active in cutting expenditure, no similar effort was made, at least until the end of the 1980's, to increase government revenues, with the result that revenues continued to decline as a share of GDP. The major factor behind this fall in total government revenues since 1986 has been the fall in oil revenues owing to the fall in oil prices, but other tax revenues, particularly from direct taxes, have also failed noticeably to rise with income.

[3] Hansen, B.: *op.cit.*, p. 18.
[4] *ibid.*, p. 18.

TABLE 2.3
Government Budget (Actual):
1983/84–1988/89
(a) Government Revenues

(in L.E. Million)

	1983/84	84/85	85/86	86/87	87/88	88/89*
1. Suez Canal	448	412	481	465	580	555
2. Petroleum	1,414	1,336	1,540	1,112	1,252	1,329
3. Other Profit Taxes	994	1,216	1,535	1,504	1,820	2,275
4. Personal Income Taxes	129	177	303	302	354	442
5. Customs Duties	1,920	1,907	1,808	1,929	2,378	2,800
6. Consumption Duties	1,302	1,444	1,489	1,722	1,984	2,450
7. Investment Self Financing	1,628	2,011	2,347	3,041	3,571	3,600
8. Other Revenues	2,535	2,810	3,289	3,424	4,044	4,592
Total Revenues	10,370	11,313	12,792	13,499	15,983	18,043

(b) Government Expenditure

(in L.E. million)

	1983/4	1984/5	1985/6	1986/7	1987/8	1988/9*
1. Defence	2,120	2,385	2,646	2,734	2,986	3,285
2. Civilian Wages & Salaries	2,620	3,158	3,446	3,691	4,570	5,265
3. Subsidies	2,609	2,749	2,766	2,270	2,717	2,993
4. Interest	1,111	1,253	1,538	1,843	2,304	3,362
5. Investment(1)	5,518	6,556	7,761	8,924	11,022	10,400
6. Other Expenditure	2,559	2,383	2,369	2,675	3,213	4,149
Total Expenditure	16,537	18,484	20,526	21,237	26,832	29,454
Overall Deficit	6,166	7,173	7,733	7,738	10,849	11,411
as % of GDP	22	22	22	18	20	17
External Financing (Net)	1,052	1,530	1,296	1,831	2,499	988

(1) Foreign currency computed by the Egyptian government at $1 = LE 0.70 in earlier years and increasingly revalued to commercial rates after 1985/86.
Source: IMF Report, January 1990, Table (1).
(*) estimated.

Deficient covering of taxable incomes, excessive exemptions, insufficiently progressive tax structure, week tax administration and laxity in tax collections have all contributed to the meagre revenues from direct taxation. In fact, only few countries in the same range of per capita income as Egypt collected less revenue than Egypt did in 1990 from taxes on incomes, profit and capital gains, as percentage of total government current revenue. This percentage was 15.9% in Egypt compared to 28.3% in Philippines, 29.5% in Syria, 45.2% in Cameron and 56.9% in Ecuador.[5] The Egyptian government continues to rely on indirect taxes as the main source of increasing its revenues, and this has become particularly evident since the introduction of the sales tax in 1991. While admittedly easier to collect, less costly to administer, and not always regressive, indirect taxes continue to dominate government revenues in Egypt as in many other Third World countries mainly because of the political obstacles in the way of increasing direct taxes.

A factor that has significant effect on both the expenditure and the revenue sides of government finance, greatly depressing the rate of saving but often ignored, is corruption. Gunnar Myrdal has long ago warned againt its neglect, and lamented the fact that "it is possible to read hundreds of books and articles on underdevelopment and development without even encountering the word 'corruption'." Myrdal does not cite Egypt as an example although much of what he says about the "soft state" in underdeveloped countries is highly relevant to Egypt, including his reference to tax laws being "deliberately written in such unclear terms that the scope for tax avoidance is increased", to "escaping taxes (being) facilitated by astonishingly lenient penalties and by keeping the administration for tax assessment and tax collection too small and not competent enough, (and) the low salaries of the officials (increasing) the possibilities of bribery."[6]

Highly relevant to the wastes of public consumption is the recent study by Yehia Sadovsky of the relationship between Egyptian businessmen and state bureaucrats.[7] He concludes that the problem of economic waste should not be simplistically reduced to a "good market, bad state" interpretation of political economy. Rather, "the quality of the relationship between these groups . . . makes a profound differ-

[5] *World Development Report*, 1990, p. 240.

[6] Myrdal, G.: *The Challenge of World Poverty*, Allen Lane, The Penguin Press, London, 1970, pp. 208–252.

[7] Sadowski, Y.: *Political Vegetables*?, The Brookings Institution, Washington D.C., 1991.

ence to a country's economic fortunes. If bureaucrats and businessmen are too hostile to each other, their feuds can do more to cripple the national economy than any natural disaster. But when bureaucrats and businessmen become allies, their collaboration can be equally debilitating. Through various forms of rent seeking, businessmen can divert public resources to their private benefit, feeding their profits without producing economic growth (much less development)."[8] His book is rich with examples of such a relationship between Egyptian businessmen and Egyptian bureaucrats.

2.3 *Private Consumption*

A remarkable feature of the development of private consumption over the last three decades is that it continued to be virtually constant as a proportion of GDP, until the mid 1980's when it showed a sudden and regular increase until now. Table 2.4 shows that the share of private consumption in GDP fluctuated within a very narrow range (63%–68%) for the whole period of thirty years, between 1955 and 1985, during which fluctuations in the rate of saving, particularly the

TABLE 2.4
Share of Private Consumption in GDP
at Current Market Prices (1955/56–1991/2)

1955/56	60/61	65/66	66/67	67/68	68/69	69/70	70/71
67.6	68.3	66.6	66.6	68.1	68.2	65.5	66.2
1971/72	73	74	75	76	77	78	82
65.1	63.8	68.4	67.7	65.2	63.2	64.6	67.0
1983	84	85	86	87	88	89	91/92
65.0	64.6	66.3	68.9	78.6	78.9	80.1	88.5

Sources: For 1955–56 to 1978, Ikram, K.: *Egypt: Economic Management in a Period of Transition*, Johns Hopkins University Press, Baltimore, 1980, pp. 396–7; for 1982–89, Table (2.2) above, and for 1991/92: Ministry of Planning: *Preliminary Framework of the Third Five-Year Plan (1992/93–1996/97)*, (in Arabic), February 1992, vol. I, p. 167.

[8] *ibid.*, pp. 315–6.

TABLE 2.5
Rates of Birth, Death and
Natural Increase in Population
(1952–1990)

(per 1000)

Year	1952	60	66	76	77	78	79	80	81
Birth Rate	45.2	42.9	40.9	36.6	37.5	37.4	40.2	37.5	37.0
Death Rate	17.8	16.9	15.8	11.8	11.8	10.5	10.9	10.0	10.0
Natural Rate of Increase in Population	27.4	26.0	25.1	24.8	25.7	26.9	29.2	27.5	27.0

Year	82	83	84	85	86	87	88	89	90
Birth Rate	36.2	36.8	38.6	39.8	38.7	37.4	36.6	33.3	32.2
Death Rate	10.0	9.7	9.5	9.4	9.2	9.1	8.1	8.1	7.5
Natural Rate of Increase in Population	26.2	27.1	29.1	30.3	29.5	28.3	28.5	25.2	24.7

Source: Central Agency for Public Mobilization and Statistics: *Statistical Year Book*, June 1991, p. 24.

drop between 1967 and 73, have to be explained mainly by changes in government consumption.

From 1985 onwards, the share of private consumption in GDP started to increase, and from 1987 quite significantly, until it reached as much as 88.5% in 1991/92. Population growth is of no help as an explanation for this increase in the rate of growth of private consumption since the rate of growth of population has shown little variation over the last four decades (see Table 2.5). The explanation may in fact be more sociological than economic or demographic, for it may be noted that the big rise in the share of private consumption occured after a fairly extended period of very high rates of growth of income (1977–84) coinciding with rising oil prices and labour remittances. It is reasonable to suppose that a good proportion of the population obstinately tried to maintain the high levels of consumption attained during the late 1970's and early 1980's even after the decline in the rate of growth of income from 1985 onwards. This recalls to mind the old hypothesis of J. Deusenberry of the existence of a "ratchet effect" whereby consumers tend to adjust their consumption more easily upwards than downwards, resisting the reduction of their consumption standards during depressions and continuing to maintain those standards acquired during the previous boom period.[9] This resistence to reducing consumption during depressions is likely to be stronger in cases where consumption levels are strongly tied with considerations of prestige, social status and such powerful psychological factors.

There is strong evidence that such considerations may have been very much at work in Egypt since the mid 1970's. Although social mobility proceeded at a high rate after the 1952 revolution, there are strong reasons to believe that it continued at a much higher rate after the mid 1970's. In addition to the expansion of education as a channel for social advancement which was already a powerful factor of social mobility in the 1950's and 1960's, there was now the even more powerful factor of external migration. Although the rate of external migration started to rise towards the late 1960's, migration did not start to contribute significantly to social mobility until the mid 1970's. Since then, the structure of Egyptian migrants started to be dominated by unskilled and semi-skilled construction workers, craftsmen and agricultural labourers who were suddenly offered unprecedented opportunities of social advancement. In contrast to other channels of social mobility, labour migration had the unique feature of requiring very little education and hardly any capital. Migration contributed indirectly, but also significantly to social mobility by raising the real income of a large number of craftsmen, construction workers and agricultural labourers who were not among the migrants, but benefitted greatly from labour shortages created by migration. The point worth emphasizing here is that the rapid increase in private consumption associated with these rising incomes, did not merely fulfil the simple function of satisfying certain consumption needs but served a much more important function as a symbol of social advancement. Thus, to these newly rising classes, the private motor car is not simply a means of transport but, perhaps more importantly, a status symbol declaring their ascendance to a higher social class. Much of the increase in luxury imports and the resulting burden on the balance of payments can similarly be attributed not merely to an increase in income but to the increase in social mobility associated with it. Even the increase in the consumption and imports of some basic foodstuffs can be explained in the same way, for a rise in the

[9] Deusenberry, J.: *Income, Saving and the Theory of Consumer Behavior*, Harvard University Press, 1949.

consumption of such necessities as rice, meat and even wheat could serve the same social function for the lower income rural households as that served by consumer durables for the urban or higher income rural population.[10]

This relationship between the increase in consumption and social mobility could go a long way towards explaining the "ratchet effect" whereby consumers find it much easier to raise their consumption expenditure when income rises than to lower it as income falls. For what is involved here is not merely the enjoyment of less goods and services but the more painful loss of prestige and social status. The big rise in the share of private consumption in GDP after 1985 may be largely attributed to this factor.

Acceleration of the rate of social mobility may also shed some light on the problem of the high rate of tax evasion. One may argue that there is a big difference between the attitude towards the state, of the old class of big landowners and industrialists who constituted the main tax payers in pre-1952 Egypt, and that of the new classes who made their fortune in the 1970's whether from migration, trade, real estate, or from land speculation. One may expect the former classes to have a stronger sense of loyalty and to feel more indebted to the state, which provided them with the necessary infrastructure, invested on their behalf in irrigation and drainage projects and enforced the law and order necessary for the protection of their interests. In contrast, much of the new income and wealth which accumulated in the 1970's may be attributed not to state activities but rather to its inactivity: to the merely passive role of the state in allowing people to migrate, and to its failure to regulate the rate of inflation and the pattern of investment. If readiness to pay one's taxes has any relationship to the sense of indebtedness to the state, the newly rising classes in Egypt would indeed be expected to show a much higher propensity to evade taxation than the older classes of taxpayers whose income came from agriculture and industry. The same weakening in the sense of loyalty to the state could also be expected from members of the legislative councils in the 1970's who increasingly came from this same class of *nouveaux riches* and who had

[10] For an elaboration of the causes and impact of accelerated social mobility in Egypt after 1975, see Amin, G.: "Migration, Inflation and Social Mobility", in Tripp, Charles and Owen, R. (eds.): *Egypt Under Mubarak*, Routledge, London, 1989, pp. 103–121.

no interest in patching up loopholes in the tax laws. It is also quite possible that the attitude towards the payment of taxes of someone whose taxable income is relatively recent, unreliable and irregular, and whose newly acquired income has served to raise him to a higher social class, would be very different from the attitude of another, whose soucre of income is long established and more secure, and whose social standing would not change significantly with an increase in income or wealth. While to the latter, the payment of taxes may be like dispensing with some extra fat of the body, to the former it may seem like giving away part of the flesh. But in periods of rapid social mobility, the propensity to evade taxes may be just as strong in the declining classes, who have every reason to resist an additional sacrifice that would only hasten their decline, especially as they see their new rivals, whom they regard as unworthy of their new wealth, unwilling to make a similar sacrifice. To these declining classes may belong a good proportion of tax collectors whose worsening social status makes them more amenable to the acceptance of gifts and bribes and whose self-confidence tend to be undermined by the increasing aggressiveness of the rising classes whose increasing defiance of the law seems to meet with the compliance and protection of the state itself.[11]

2.4 *Capital Flight*

A major economic problem that has acquired serious proportions over the last twenty years and has led the recorded rate of savings, the rate of actual domestic investment as well as the ability to service the external debt to be much less than would have been otherwise, is the problem of capital flight. Estimates of capital flight from Egypt vary widely and it is not always clear whether the estimates include capital transferred from Egypt or savings realized by Egyptians abroad but not transferred back to Egypt. The latter has been estimated at as much as $63 billion for the period 1975–89,[12] but estimates which also include transfers from Egypt sometimes approach twice this figure.

Explanations given for capital flight from Egypt, as well as the

[11] See Amin, G.: *op.cit.*, pp. 114–5.

[12] Besada, Raafat Shafik: *Egyptians Working abroad*, (Arabic), General Egyptian Book Organization, Cairo, 1991, p. 57.

reluctance of Egyptians working abroad to transfer a greater proportion of their savings to Egypt, include the overvalued exchange rate, negative rates of interest on deposits in Egyptian banks, uncertainty of investment climate, bureaucratic obstacles and the frequent changing of laws governing investment in Egypt. While all these factors are certainly responsible for part of the problem and point to some economic policy measures that could be taken to encourage the repatriation of such funds, other factors may also be involved, could be more important and are less amenable to manipulation by economic policy makers. Ramzy Zaki[13] has rightly pointed out that much of the capital flight from Egypt is the result of illegal earnings which are searching not as much for higher rates of return abroad as for a place of hiding. All types of corruption and illegitimate activities could be involved including the sheer desire to escape taxation. This is one reason, of course, why economic reform by itself cannot be relied upon to guarantee the reverse flow of funds back to Egypt and why it may be useful to distinguish, as Zaki suggests, between the "flight" and the "smuggling" of capital, each requiring a very different set of policies.

2.5 *Foreign Investment*

The big fall in the rate of national saving following the 1967 war was a major factor in the reorientation of Egypt's economic policy towards a more liberal attitude towards private foreign investment. After two decades of hostility to foreign investment, following the nationalization of the Suez Canal in 1956, and during which an extremely narrow domain was allowed for foreign investment, mainly in the oil sector, Law 43 of 1974 for Foreign and Arab Investment and Free Zones inaugrated the new era of open-door policy, one of its main features being the encouragement of private foreign investment. Law 43, together with its amendments by Law 32 of 1977, extended generous tax holidays to foreign investors, liberal terms for capital and profit transfers, exemptions from labour laws, from exchange control regulations and from import and export licenses as well as guarantees against nationalization. The amendment of 1977 provided foreign investors with additional incentives in the form of a

[13] In the June symposium referred to above.

more favourable exchange rate in the transfer of capital, and allowed foreign investors to buy foreign currencies in the local market. Both Law 43 and its 1977 amendment have again been replaced by the even more generous Law 230 of 1989 extending further the periods of tax holidays, and allowing foreign ownership of land and real estate which was previously prohibited.

The latest law of 1989 is too recent to allow an assessment of its impact, but there is sufficient data to evaluate the impact of the earlier laws. In terms of the number of projects approved and the magnitude of their total cost, in application to Law 43 and its 1977 amendment, the result has not been insignificant. According to the Investment Authority responsible for the supervision of the implementation of this law, by mid 1989, a total of 1427 inland projects (to be distinguished from those of the Free Zones) have been approved, with a cumulative authorized capital of L.E. 7.5 billion and total investment cost (which includes this plus loans) of L.E. 14 billion.[14]

Actual implementation fell short of what had been approved so that by 1989, two-thirds of the number of projects approved (representing 57% of the total investment costs of approved projects) were in operation and another 13% (representing 17% of total investment cost) were under execution. In spite of this considerable lag of actual implementation behind the approval of projects, the share of implemented Law 43 projects in the total gross fixed investment in Egypt has not been small and their share in total private sector investment has been impressive. It has been calculated that over the period 1977–1986/87, total Law 43 investments (in current prices) accounted for about 10% of total fixed gross investment and 41% of that of the private sector. The contribution of Law 43 projects to imports of capital goods has also been significant. For the period 1975–1984/85, these projects accounted for 13% of the total imports of capital goods to Egypt and 41% of total private sector (excluding petroleum) imports of capital goods (see Table 2.6).

The important thing to note here is that, although Law 43 and its amendments had aimed mainly at attracting private foreign investment, the "foreign" component in its projects has been far lower

---

[14] Handoussa, H.: "Egypt's Investment Strategy, Policies and Performance since the Infitah", in El-Naggar, S. (ed.) *Investment Policies in Arab Countries*, the Arab Fund for Economic and Social Development and the Arab Monetary Fund, (Arabic edition), Kuwait 1989, p. 349.

TABLE 2.6
Distribution of Imports of Capital Goods by Importing Companies (1975–1984/85)

Imports	$ Billion	%
Foreign Petroleum Companies	5.53	22
Law 43 Projects	3.28	13
Other Private Sector Companies	4.74	19
Public Sector	11.87	46
Total	25.42	100

Source: Handoussa, *op.cit.*, p. 353.

than was originally hoped. One of the main purposes of the amendment of Law 43 made by Law 32 of 1977 was to provide equal treatment of Egyptian and foreign capital so long as both participated with foreign currency. The end result was that most of the capital provided by the investment made according to the laws encouraging "foreign" investment, was in fact "Egyptian". This is one important conclusion of H. Esfahani's study of the experience of foreign investment in Egypt since 1974.[15] Table 2.7 below also shows that since 1977, the share of foreign capital (including non-Egyptian Arab) in inland investments has shown a regular decline, from 50% in 1977 to 33% in 1989. The share of foreign capital in investments in the Free Zones has been greater and showed some increase, but even here the cumulative share of Egyptian capital has been more than a third in 1989.

Thus, distinguishing between the total response to the laws encouraging foreign investment and the response of *foreign* capital, it turns out that while total equity capital received under Law 43 up to the end of June 1989 amounted to $5112.2 million, non-Egyptian participation amounted only to $1850 million. If financial capital is excluded, non-Egyptian participation would fall to $1019 million.[16] This is less than one-tenth of the total Egyptian imports of goods and services in one year (1988/89) and less than the interest on external debt paid by Egypt in the same year ($1123).

It is interesting to speculate on the possible reasons for this disap-

[15] Esfahani, Hadi: *The Experience of Foreign Investment in Egypt under Infitah*, Faculty Working Paper, College of Commerce and Business Administration, University of Illinois at Urbana-Champaign, December 1990.

[16] *ibid.*, pp. 13–14.

TABLE 2.7
Participation of Countries in the Cumulative Capital of Projects Approved under Law 43
(Percentages)

Year	Egypt	Arab Countries	United States	E.E.C. Countries	Other Countries	Total
Inland						
1977	50	24	6		20[a]	100
1979	55	17	9	5	14	100
1980	58	12	8	8	14	100
1982	61	23	4	5	7	100
1984	71	15	4	6	4	100
1985	–	–	–	–	–	–
1986	71	14		15[b]		100
1987	70	14	5	6	5	100
1988	–	–	–	–	–	100
1989	67	16		17[b]		100
Free Zones						
1984	38	31	7	6	18	100
1987	31	47	6	5	11	100
1988	–	–				100
1989	35	43		22[b]		100

(a) for E.E.C. and "other countries".
(b) for U.S., E.E.C. and "other countries".
Source: Esfahani, Hadi: *The Experience of Foreign Investment in Egypt under Infitah*, Faculty Working Paper, College of Commerce and Business Administration, University of Illinois at Urbana-Champaign, December, 1990.

pointing performance of *foreign* investment in Egypt over the last two decades. It is very unlikely that the cause is to be found in the lack of incentives provided by Law 43, which is generally regarded as quite generous in the treatment of foreign investors. Nor is red tape or the lack of interest on the part of the Egyptian government to carry the major blame, since procedures have tended to be progressively simplified while foreign participation has shown a tendency to decline over the 1980's. Available data on investment costs of approved projects under Law 43 show a marked increase in 1979/80–1981/82 to be followed by a big decline, particularly since 1985/86. As Esfahani rightly points out, what seems to have been more decisive in influencing private foreign investment in Egypt is the foreign investor's assessment of Egypt's economic prospects and particularly the prospects of the balance of payments.[17] The late 1970's and early

[17] See Esfahani, *op.cit.*, pp. 26–32.

1980's were the years of the Camp David agreements and of the big surge in foreign exchange receipts as a result of rising oil prices. The mid 1980's witnessed the beginning of a big deterioration in the balance of payments which was aggravated by the big fall in oil prices in 1986. Private foreign investment seems to have been more sensitive to such factors than to the degree of leniency of investment laws. A deterioration in the external debt situation and a decline in the ability to service it seems to be more decisive as a disincentive to foreign investors than the lack of tax exemptions. Rather than relying on private foreign investment to reduce the burden of external debt, it is therefore the reduction of the burden of debt which seems to be an important condition for encouraging foreign investment.

2.6 *Foreign Aid*

It is now 17 years since the Western World, as well as the World Bank and the International Monetary Fund resumed their economic assistance to Egypt, after a period of about 10 years during which the flow of Western aid into Egypt had declined to an insignificant amount. Since 1975, economic as well as military assistance has been flowing into Egypt at a startling rate, particularly from the U.S.A. After its complete suspension in February 1967 for about 7 years, U.S. aid to Egypt started to flow again from 1975 onwards, and at an increasing rate until Egypt became one of the biggest recipients of American aid per capita, and the U.S. became Egypt's biggest creditor as well as its largest trade partner. Over the 14-year period (1975–88), the annual average of U.S. total economic aid commitments to Egypt was no less than $1 billion.

Associated with this rapid increase in American aid to Egypt was also a rapid increase in the aid provided by other western countries, multilateral institutions as well as bilateral and multilateral aid from Arab countries and institutions. Taking all these sources of funds, in addition to American aid, the annual average flow of gross disbursements of civilian loans to Egypt during 1975–87 amounts to $2128 million (see Table 2.8 below). This sum, which excludes grants as well as military lending, far exceeds any flow of funds that Egypt had ever known, and is about 10 times the annual level of both loans and grants to Egypt during the period of ambitious development efforts of the 1960's ($217 million annually during 1956–66).[18] The major contributors to this flow since 1975, after the U.S., have been the countries of Western Europe, Japan and Canada, followed by Arab countries and the World Bank group, as is roughly indicated by the distribution of Egypt's external debt by creditor in 1986 (see Table 1.1 above).

TABLE 2.8
Gross Disbursements of External Loans from all Sources to Egypt (1975–1987)

(million $)

1975	2541	1981/82	2603
76	1520	82/83	2491
77	2894	83/84	2253
78	2278	84/85	2019
79	2126	85/86	2519
1980/81	2408	86/87	1406

Sources: *1975–1981/82*: World Bank: *Arab Republic of Egypt: Current Economic Situation and Growth Prospects*, Oct. 1983, p. 42.
1981/82–86/87: World Bank: *Arab Republic of Egypt: Country Economic Memorandum, Economic Readjustment With Growth*, Sept. 1988, p. 83.

Foreign aid to Egypt, as for other third world countries has been subject to many criticisms; one of which is that too great a proportion of it consisted of military aid. Just before the exemption from U.S. military debt in 1991, military debt constituted about one-fourth of Egypt's total external debt, and Egypt's military debt to the U.S. constituted more than a third of Egypt's total debt to that country. This should have been not a little surprising almost twenty years after President Sadat declared the 1973 war to be "the last war". Even when military aid is given as a grant, it creates an additional burden on the economy in the form of new expenditure, in both local and foreign currencies, which would have not been incurred otherwise. If aid disbursements rather than aid commitments are taken into account, the share of military aid in total aid extended to Egypt

[18] It is interesting to note from the figures of Table 2.8 the fairly regular character of the total flow of external lending to Egypt between the mid 1970's and mid 1980's, in spite of the sudden suspension of Arab aid to Egypt after the signing of the Camp David and peace agreements with Israel in 1979 and 1979.

becomes significantly larger. Table 2.9 below shows that with regard to U.S. economic aid to Egypt during the 11-year period (1975–85), commitments were as much as 35% larger than disbursements.

TABLE 2.9
U.S. Economic Aid to Egypt
(1975–1988)

	1 Project Aid(c)	2 CIP(1) (c)	3(1+2) ESF(2)(**) (c)	4 ESF(2) (d)	5 PL480 (c)	6(1+2+5) Total (c)
1975	85	150	235	25	111	346
76	458	314	772	94	192	964
77	245	437	682	167	193	875
78	429	297	726	523	189	915
79	472	334	814	367	230	1044
80	510	334	844	605	299	1143
81	506	300	806	737	298	1104
82	412	350	762	597	292	1054
83	447	301	748	868	258	1006
84	450	402*	852	905	264	1116
85	515	550*	1065	1272	236	1301
86	553	515*	1068	n/a	219	1287
87	n/a	n/a	806	n/a	171	977
88	n/a	n/a	705	n/a	171	876

(1) CIP = Commodity Import Program
(2) ESF = Economic Support Fund
(*) Cash transfers of $102 million, $350 million and $360 million are included for the three years 1984, 1985 and 1986 consecutively.
(**) Economic Support Fund = Project Aid + Commodity Import Program
(c) Commitment
(d) Disbursement
Source: Handoussa, H.: *15 Years of U.S. Aid to Egypt*, a paper submitted to the 13th annual symposium, Center for Contemporary Arab Studies, Georgetown University, April 14–15, 1988, (mimeo.), p. 5.

It has also been noted that a not insignificant proportion (12%) of U.S. project aid to Egypt has gone to finance consultancy services performed by American firms at excessively high cost. Two examples of this are mentioned in a report prepared by the Central Agency for Auditing (of government accounts) in the mid 1980's, concerning two American loans for the rehabilitation of the Alexandria sewage system and the development of the Port of Suez, where 59.5% of the amount of the first loan and 43.3% of the second were paid as fees to foreign consultant firms.[19]

[19] Central Agency for Auditing: *Report on Egypt's External Indebtedness on 30 June 1984 and Policies Affecting it*, (Arabic), not dated, mimeographed, p. 90.

The benefit to Egypt of foreign loans is further reduced to the extent that the loan is tied to purchases from specific sources which may be unjustifiably more costly than other sources. The same government report just quoted referred to a letter from the Egyptian Ministry of Industry dated 12/2/85 complaining that American goods financed by U.S. loans are sometimes twice as expensive as similar goods available elsewhere. The same report complained that U.S. loan agreements stipulate that the transportation of a certain proportion of the goods financed by the loan be through American shipping companies, the cost of which could sometimes reach four times the prevailing cost of shipping.

All the above criticisms, however, amount to saying in one way or another that the magnitude of foreign aid is not big enough or, because of certain leakages, is not as big as it may seem. More important perhaps than the mere size of aid is the fact that foreign aid to Egypt, like private foreign investment, seems to have been governed more by political considerations and by the ability to repay than by economic need.

Tracing the development of foreign aid to Egypt over the last three decades one notes that Western aid declined heavily during the period between the two wars of 1967 and 1973, mainly because of political reasons and in spite of Egypt's dire need for economic assistance at that time. Both U.S. economic aid (see Table 2.9) and total external loans (see Table 2.8) continued at a high level after the 1979 peace treaty with Israel, at a time when the great flow of foreign exchange from oil and labour remittances made Egypt in little need for aid. After 1986, however, when Egypt was in greater need than ever for external assistance, the flow of American and total aid declined either in response to the increasing economic difficulties themselves, or as a way of pressuring Egypt to accept the measures proposed by the international finance institutions, or perhaps for both reasons. Thus, as we have seen with private foreign investment, it seems that rather than foreign lending being a way of helping to cope with balance of payments difficulties, it may be necessary to have a healthy balance of payments in order to be able to obtain much foreign lending.

CHAPTER THREE

THE RENTIER ECONOMY

3.1 *A Rentier Economy?*

For about 15 years now, the four largest single contributors of foreign exchange to Egypt have been oil, labour remittances, the Suez Canal and tourism. All together reached a peak of 75% of Egypt's total current receipts of foreign exchange in 1981/2, and although this proportion has declined since then, particularly after the big fall in oil prices in 1986, it still is no less than 60% (see tables 3.1 and 3.2). Before 1975, the picture was very different, with cotton exports (including yarn and textiles) bringing substantially more than any of these four items. Revenues from oil, tourism and the Suez Canal had been severely affected by the 1967 war, while workers' remittances from abroad had not yet started to become a significant source of foreign exchange, bringing even less than tourism.[1]

It has often been remarked, and quite correctly, that each of these four sources of income contains a big element of "economic rent", a good part of it being largely unrelated to effort, and variations in it reflecting much more the changes in demand conditions than in cost.

There is nothing necessarily "shameful" about an economy deriving much of its sustenance from rent, and realizing incomes that are unrelated to effort, even if this is so with regard to individuals. But such an economy faces certain dangers that may not be present, to the same extent, in other economies, and this is certainly so in the case of Egypt. All the four sources of income are more influenced by demand conditions than by supply, and there is relatively limited scope here for adjusting supply to cope with an increase or a decrease in demand when compared, say, with manufactured exports. Moreover, demand in the case of at least three of these four sources of income is more subject to the influence of political factors than other exports, adding more sources of instability of income, and

[1] See Ikram, K., *op.cit.*, pp. 342 and 349.

at least in the two cases of oil and Suez Canal revenues, there seems to be less scope for influencing demand by economic policy than in the case of agricultural or manufactured exports.

Fluctuations in Egypt's economic fortune during the last quarter of a century indeed testify to all this. The 1967 war had disastrous effects on the Egyptian economy largely because of its effect on revenues from oil, the Suez Canal and tourism. The recovery after 1975 was largely due to the same factors working in the opposite direction, in addition to the rise in oil prices in 1973, 1974, 1979 and 1980. The downturn after 1985 has been again largely due to the fall in oil prices, while tourism and workers' remittances have been affected indirectly by the fluctuations in oil prices, since a good part of tourists visiting Egypt are from oil-rich countries and workers' remittances are predominantly from the same countries. Tourist revenues have also been sensitive to domestic as well as regional political events.

The Gulf crisis of 1990/91 was only the most recent example of how dependent the Egyptian economy has become on a variety of "rent incomes" that are subject to factors over which Egypt has little control. With the eruption of the crisis in August 1990, a major balance-of-payments crisis was anticipated since the three major sources of foreign exchange, other than oil, were expected to suffer greatly, while the expected rise in oil prices did not seem likely to compensate sufficiently for this loss. Estimates of the expected loss varied widely. Early in 1991, the Egyptian government estimated the total impact of the crisis on the balance of payments at $5.9 billion in 1990/91, several Western analysts estimated the total loss in the balance of payments to be closer to $2 billion, while the World Bank predicted Egypt's losses to be about $1.2 billion in the calender year 1990, and another $2 billion in 1991. Although this estimate of $3.2 billion was considerably smaller than the estimate of the Egyptian government, it was equal to the total value of Egypt's commodity exports in 1989/90 and as much as 25% of all of Egypt's receipts of foreign exchange in that year, other than official transfers. To everybody's surprise, not only did the impact of the crisis turn out to be much lighter than expected, but the balance of current accounts in 1990/91 actually realized a surplus of $1391.3 million, which represents an improvement of $2605.2 over the previous year (see Table 3.3). The increase in revenues from oil exports was less than

TABLE 3.1
Egyptian Balance of Current Transactions (1981/82 – 1989/90)

(U.S. $ million)

	1981/2	82/3	83/4	84/5	85/6	86/7	87/8	88/9	89/90
Receipts:									
Proceeds of Exports	3846.6	3741.9	3960.4	3927.8	3575.7	2264.4	3274.0	2737.5	3206.1
of which Petroleum	3329.0	2807.0	2957.0	2891.0	2210.0	1364.0	1532.0	1240.0	1229.0
Shipping	531.1	602.2	562.6	606.0	574.0	508.1	446.6	533.7	535.9
Suez Canal Dues	908.9	956.6	974.0	896.7	1028.3	1148.0	1268.7	1306.7	1471.8
Tourism	392.8	304.1	288.4	409.6	315.3	379.6	885.9	900.6	1066.6
Interest, Dividends & Other Revenues	468.0	473.7	545.6	567.5	534.3	613.5	624.1	734.0	775.7
Other Receipts	658.3	1079.6	1064.3	1025.6	992.3	1367.0	1349.3	1582.7	1729.7
Total	6805.8	7158.1	7395.3	7433.2	7019.9	6280.6	7848.6	7795.2	8785.8
Payments:									
Payments for Imports	8618.2	8269.3	9519.3	9640.6	8554.1	7323.3	9841.0	10293.5	10773.2
Commercial Payments	147.1	113.1	119.4	129.3	136.5	197.2	204.5	248.0	271.2
Shipping	143.0	135.0	174.0	159.0	218.4	164.8	114.5	109.4	80.8
Interest on Loans & Obligations	791.6	943.3	1048.5	818.8	1165.8	921.0	785.1	1123.2	1686.2
Travel, Education & Medical Expenses	239.2	300.1	262.3	254.9	150.2	126.5	85.6	111.8	86.8
Government Expenditures	247.3	256.0	277.0	318.4	314.7	254.5	319.6	311.8	312.4
Other Payments	1057.9	1228.4	1372.3	1391.1	1613.2	1574.1	1124.3	'1394.0	1612.8

Table 3.1 (*cont.*)

	1981/2	82/3	83/4	84/5	85/6	86/7	87/8	88/9	89/90
Total	11244.3	11245.2	12772.8	12712.1	12152.9	10561.4	12474.6	13591.7	14823.4
Balance of Current Transactions	–4438.5	–4087.1	–5377.5	–5278.9	–5133.0	–4280.8	–4626.0	–5796.5	–6037.6
Transfers:									
Official	51.0	25.6	26.1	222.1	507.4	344.6	697.5	711.2	1080.2
Workers' Remittances	2081.9	3165.4	3930.5	3496.2	2972.7	3011.9	3383.9	3532.2	3743.5
Total	2132.9	3191.0	3956.6	3718.3	3480.1	3356.5	4084.4	4243.4	4823.7
Balance of Current Transactions & Transfers	2305.6	–896.1	–1420.9	–1560.6	–1652.9	–924.3	–544.6	–1553.1	–1213.9

Sources: Central Bank of Egypt: *Annual Reports*; World Bank: *ARE, Country Economic Memorandum, Economic Readjustment with Growth*, 1990, Vol. 3 and *IMF Report*, January 1990, Table 4.

TABLE 3.2
Share of Petroleum, Suez Canal, Tourism and Workers' Remittances in Total Foreign Exchange Receipts other than Official Transfers
(1981/2–1989/90)

(U.S. $ million)	1981/2	82/3	83/4	84/5	85/6	86/7	87/8	88/9	89/90
Total Exports of Goods and Services ($ mil.)	6805.8	7158.1	7395.3	7433.2	7019.9	6280.6	7848.6	7795.2	8785.8
Workers' Remittances ($ mil.)	2081.9	3165.4	3930.5	3496.2	2972.7	3011.9	3383.9	3532.2	3743.5
Total Foreign Exchange of Current Receipts other than Official Transfer ($ mil.)	8887.7	10323.5	11325.8	10929.4	9992.6	9292.5	11232.5	11327.4	12529.3
of Which Petroleum %	37.4	27.2	26.1	26.4	22.1	14.7	13.6	10.9	9.8
Suez Canal %	10.2	9.3	8.6	8.2	10.3	12.3	11.3	11.5	11.7
Tourism %	4.4	2.9	2.5	3.7	3.1	4.1	7.9	7.9	8.5
Workers' Remittances %	23.4	30.7	34.7	32.0	29.7	32.4	30.1	31.2	29.9
Total of Four Shares	75.4	70.1	71.9	70.3	65.2	63.5	62.9	61.5	59.9

Sources: Calculated from Table 3.1

expected,[2] but neither the revenues from the Suez Canal nor labour remittances showed the expected decline. The revenues from the Suez Canal actually showed some increase (13%) due to the rise in the number of oil tankers from Saudi Arabia as a result of the increase in Saudi oil production, as well as to the passing of warships through the Canal.

TABLE 3.3
Balance of Current Transactions
in 1990/91 Compared with 1989/90

(US $ million)

	1989/1990	1990/91(*)
Receipts:		
Proceeds of Exports	3206.1	3886.8
Shipping	535.9	811.9
Suez Canal Dues	1471.8	1661.9
Tourism	1066.6	924.1
Interest, Dividends and Other Revenues	775.7	1049.4
Other Receipts	1729.7	3231.5
Total	8785.8	11565.6
Payments		
Payments for Imports	10773.2	11424.5
Commercial Payments	271.2	232.2
Shipping	80.8	101.0
Interest on Loans and Obligations	1686.2	1529.7
Travel, Education and Medical Expenses	86.8	82.9
Government Expenditure	312.4	444.7
Other Payments	1612.8	1621.5
Total	14823.4	15436.5
Balance of Current Transactions (without transfers)	−6037.6	−3770.9
Transfers		
Official	1080.2	1486.9
Workers' Remittances	3743.5	3775.3
Total	4823.7	5262.2
Balances of Current Transactions & Transfers	−1213.9	1391.3

* Preliminary figures
Source: For 1989/90: Table 3.1; for 1990/91: Central Bank of Egypt: *Annual Report, 1990/91.*

[2] $742 million compared with the increase of about $1.2 billion expected by the Minister of Oil (Report of the Central Bank presented to the Egyptian Parliament on "*The Monetary and Credit Situation during 1990/91*") (Arabic), September 1991, p. 89.

Labour remittances remained virtually constant probably as a result of the fact that Egyptian workers returning to Egypt because of the crisis, have repatriated part of their accumulated savings abroad which compensated for the decline in current transfers. Revenues from tourism also did not show the expected big decline partly as a result of the expenditure in Egypt of some 30,000 exiled Kuwaitis. The improvement was also caused by a reduction in debt-service obligations, and the big increase in official transfers, to which we have already referred,[3] and which were declared to be in recognition of Egypt's political wisdom in handling the crisis as well as the increase in the revenues from services provided by Egypt to the military operations resulting from the crisis.[4]

Both the big deterioration that had been expected in the balance of payments in the early months of the crisis, and the significant improvement actually realized a few months later, were largely determined by the development (expected or actual) of the four major sources of "rent income", in addition to foreign assistance, and both were the outcome of an unexpected political event over which Egypt had very little control. These four major sources of foreign exchange will now be examined in greater detail, to see how amenable they are to manipulation by economic policy, and how much they can be expected to contribute to the alleviation of the debt burden.

3.2 *Labour Remittances*

Since 1978, labour remittances have been the largest single source of foreign exchange to Egypt, with the exception only of the three years following the big rise in oil prices in 1979. During the last few years, they have constituted no less than 30% of all of Egypt's receipts of foreign exchange excluding official transfers, far exceeding the contribution of oil since the big fall in oil prices in the mid 1980's. However, neither the big role of remittances in sustaining the balance of current accounts, nor their fluctuations from year to year, could be attributed in any great measure to deliberate economic policies, both being largely the result of individual responses to changing external conditions or to political developments at home.

---

[3] See Chapter One.

[4] Central Bank Report to Parliament, *op.cit.*, p. 90.

The emergence of labour remittances in the mid 1970's, as a contributor of some significance to foreign exchange receipts, was the direct result of the sudden increase in oil revenues in the Gulf countries and their launching of ambitious development programs. The fact that the Egyptian government had reduced its restrictions on travel abroad after the 1967 war, was, of course, an important but passive measure, and was motivated more by political than by economic considerations. The significant fall in remittances in 1981/82 was probably a reaction to political uncertainties following the assassination of President Sadat, while the resumption of the increase during the following two years had a lot to do with the increase in the number of Egyptian migrants to Iraq in the early years of the Iraq/Iran war. The decline and then the slackening of remittances since 1985 were largely due to the slackening of the process of migration, the increase in the number of those returning to Egypt and the restraint of expenditure in the host countries associated with the fall in oil prices (see Table 3.4).

TABLE 3.4
Annual Fluctuations in Labour Remittances
(1974–1990/91)

Year	Millions of U.S. $	% Change	Year	Millions of U.S. $	% Change
1974	189	—	83/84	3930	+24
75	366	+94	84/85	3496	–11
76	755	+106	85/86	2973	–15
77	897	+19	86/87	3012	+1
78	1761	+96	87/88	3384	+12
79	2214	+26	88/89	3532	+4
1980/81	2625	+19	89/90	3743	+6
81/82	2082	–21	1990/91	3775	+1
82/83	3165	+52			

Sources: 1974–1980/81: World Bank: A.R.E.: *Issues of Trade Strategy and Investment Planning*, January 1983, p. 412. 1981/82–1989/90: Table 3.1 above. 1990/91: Table 3.3 above.

Although the deterioration in Egyptian-Arab relationships following Sadat's visit to Jerusalem in 1977, and particularly after the Camp David agreements of 1978 and the Peace Treaty of 1979, seems to have had surprisingly little effect on Egyptian labour migration and remittances, other political developments in the region did have an important influence. The ups and downs in Egypt's relations with

Libya, Iraq and Jordan affected both the number of migrants and returnees to and from these countries, as well as the magnitude of their remittances, as was particularly notable in the remittances from Iraq just before the Iraqi invasion of Kuwait. Estimates of the number of Egyptians who returned from the Gulf countries as a result of the Iraqi invasion, range between 350,000 and 670,000.[5] Many of these have returned to the Gulf after the end of the war, with Saudi Arabia absorbing a greater number than were there before the crisis, but the constancy of the remittances between 1989/90 and 1990/91 shown in Table 3.4 is probably the result, as we have already indicated, of the transfer of capital taking the place of the fall in transfers from current income.

TABLE 3.5
Alternative Estimates of the Number of Egyptians Working in Arab Countries in 1985

('000 persons)

Host Country	Estimate of National Population Council	Estimate of ESCWA	Estimate of National Specialized Councils
S. Arabia	361	500	400
Kuwait	145	137	137
Iraq	424	1164	625
Jordan	90	130	130
Libya	33	76	(–)
Others	157	110	282
Total	1210	2117	1574

(–) not available

Source: El-Khawaga, Laila: *The Return of Egyptian Migrant Labour from Arab Oil-Producing Countries and Its Impact on the Egyptian Labour Market*, Center for Economic and Financial Studies, Faculty of Economics, Cairo University, Cairo 1989, *memo.* (in Arabic).

---

[5] The number of Egyptians working abroad is still not known with any degree of certainty. A 1989 study conducted by the Center for Economics and Financial Studies of the Faculty of Economics, Cairo University, quotes three widely different estimates for the number of Egyptians working in Kuwait and Iraq in 1985, included in Table 3.5 below, and show particularly striking differences in the case of Iraq. Another set of figures are contained in the Egyptian government's memorandum to the World Bank on the impact of the Gulf crisis, dated 24/1/1991, which again gives very different figures from those of Table 3.5, indicating as many as 850,000 Egyptians in Iraq, 340,000 in Kuwait and 150,000 in Jordan, just before the Gulf crisis. This memo then estimates the number of Egyptians returning to Egypt as a result of the crisis at 50% of the totals just given, making the total number of returnees 670,000 Egyptians, compared with about half this figure given by other

The main qualifications that have to be made regarding the relatively weak role of deliberate policies, have to do with the big increase in remittances in 1978 and the increase of 1987/88. The former was probably in reaction to the introduction of the "own-exchange import" system, the devaluation of the Egyptian pound and the application of more attractive exchange rates to remittances in 1977, and the latter was probably the reaction to the 25.6% devaluation between May 1987 and early 1988. Up to the early 1990's, however, interest rates in Egypt have been working towards discouraging rather than encouraging remittances. In fact, for most of the period between the mid 1970's, when remittances started to become significant, and 1991, both lending and deposit interest rates were negative in real terms, thus discouraging domestic savings and remittances and encouraging the holding of deposits in foreign currency and capital flight. In May 1987, domestic interest rates were raised between one and two points, and another rise of 2.3 points occurred in 1989, but real interest rates continued to be negative with the rate of inflation being around 25% and nominal interest rates on deposits not exceeding 13.25%, while deposits in U.S. dollars could bring at that time 7.8% interest. This was the situation that gave birth to the emergence and rapid spread of the phenomenon of "Islamic Investment Companies". These companies competed very successfully with commercial banks in mobilizing labour remittances by offering considerably higher interest rates (often double that offered by the banking system).

The long history of negative real interest rates approached its end in January 1991 when ceilings on deposit and lending rates were abolished, an auction in treasury bills introduced and the Central Bank discount rate fixed at two percentage points above the rate reached in the auction. Treasury bill rates thus rose to 14.25% in January 1991 and again to 18% in April of the same year. In February 1991, another important step was taken regarding the foreign exchange system, whereby the three-tier exchange regime (a Central Bank pool with subsidized rates for essential imports, a commercial bank pool with rates set by a bank committee and a quasi-legal parallel market with rates determined by market forces) was replaced by a transitional two-tier structure consisting of primary and secondary

sources (see for instance: The Economist Intelligence Unit: *Country Report, Egypt*, December 2, 1990 which estimates the number of Egyptian returnees at 350,000).

exchange markets, the former replacing the Central Bank pool and the latter being a new free market. Labour remittances were now subject to the latter market, i.e. to an exchange rate determined freely by market forces. The primary market where rates were to be maintained within 5% of the average prevailing daily market rate, was supposed to be merged into the free market after twelve months but was actually merged sooner, in October 1991, when the exchange market was finally unified.

The 1991 measures are too recent for their impact on remittances to be assessed, in addition to them being taken in the middle of the Gulf crisis when other important factors were at work. But with both the exchange rate and interest rates finally freed from administrative control, economic policy measures that still remain available for influencing the magnitude of remittances are few and perhaps much less effective. A World Bank report has recently referred to some rough estimates indicating that Egyptian workers abroad save at least $2.3 billion more per year than what they actually transfer home.[6] Many suggestions have been made with the aim of increasing the number and earning capacity of migrants through specially-designed educational and training measures, increasing their earnings through special agreements with host countries, or enhancing the proportion of their income which is transferred home either by taxation or by offering them attractive exchange and interest rates or specially-designed investment opportunities. While all such measures are worthy of examination, the history of the last two decades indicate that political factors are likely to have the more decisive influence on remittances. Many of these suggested economic policy measures are themselves unlikely to be possible in the absence of certain political conditions. This is particularly obvious in the case of reaching new agreements with host countries on the treatment of expatriate labour. The most decisive factor, however, seems to be how many migrants are allowed in the host countries in the first place. This is primarily dependent on the political relationships between the two countries as well as on the political orientation of the host countries over which, at least within the Arab political climate prevailing at present and in the foreseeable future, economic policy makers have little control.

The new five-year plan (1992/3–1996/7) apparently recognizes this limited scope for influencing the future of remittances and hence adopts

---

[6] World Bank: *A.R.E.: Economic Readjustment with Growth*, 1990, vol. 2, p. 46.

a conservative estimate of its growth during the plan years. Giving an estimate of remittances for 1991/92 of LE 12,646 million, which implies that remittances remained virtually constant between 90/91 and 91/92 in spite of the foreign exchange and interest rate measures of 1991, the plan envisages an annual growth rate for remittances in real terms of only 1.2% (see Table 3.6). From what was said above, this caution seems justified.

TABLE 3.6
Balance of Current Transactions
in the Five-Year Plan (1992/3–1996/7)

(A) *Receipts*

	Value in L.E. million at 1991/92 prices		
	1991/92 (Estimate)	1996/97 (Planned)	Annual Growth Rate (%)
Commodity Exports:			
Agricultural Exports	1575	2480	9.5
Manufactured Exports	5762	12125	16.0
Petroleum & Its Products	5545	4349	(4.7)
Share of Foreign Partner	1557	1793	2.9
Exports in Return for Petroleum Investment	2266	2645	3.1
Total Commodity Exports	16705	23392	7.0
Exports of Services:			
Insurance	144	178	4.3
Shipping	2090	2290	1.8
Suez Canal	5829	7236	4.4
Tourism	4690	7873	10.9
Other Services	9983	11558	3.0
Total Exports of Services	22736	29135	5.1
Factor Services:			
Workers' Remittances	12646	13400	1.2
Interest, Dividends & Other Revenues	2466	2930	3.5
Total Factor Services	15112	16330	1.6
Transfers:			
Transfers to Individuals & Private Institutions	827	883	1.3
Transfers to Government	3685	1000	(23.0)
Total Transfers	4512	1883	(16.0)
Total Current Transactions	59065	70740	3.7

TABLE 3.6 (*cont.*)
(B) *Payments*

	Value in L.E. million at 1991/92 prices		
	1991/92 (Estimate)	1996/97 (Planned)	Annual Growth Rate (%)
Commodity Imports:			
Consumer Goods	10810	11325	0.9
Intermediate Goods	18150	21355	3.3
Capital Goods	11240	12295	1.8
Total Commodity Imports	40200	44975	2.3
Imports of Services:			
Insurance	124	140	2.5
Shipping	412	462	2.3
Tourism	385	470	4.1
Government Expenditure	1598	1810	2.5
Other Payments	5720	6633	3.0
Return for Petroleum Investment	2266	2645	3.1
Total Imports of Services	10505	12160	3.0
Factor Services:			
Interest on Loans & Obligations	4690	7500	9.8
Other Payments	470	549	3.2
Share of Foreign Partner	1557	1793	2.9
Total Factor Services	6717	9842	7.9
Transfers:	3	3	—
Total Current Transactions	57425	66980	3.1
Balance of Trade	−23495	−21583	−1.7
Balance of Services	12231	16975	6.8
Balance of Current Transactions	−11264	−4608	−16.4
Net Factor Services	8395	6488	−5.0
Net Transfers	4509	1880	−16.1
Balance of Current Transactions & Transfers	+1640	+3760	25.8

Source: Ministry of Planning: *Preliminary Framework of the Third Five-Year Plan (1992–96/7)* (in Arabic), vol. I, Table (44).

3.3 *Oil*

Though not one of the oil-rich countries in relation to its population, Egypt's dependence on oil revenues has become, since the mid 1970's, comparable to that of the capital surplus, oil-rich countries of the Gulf. For apart from what Egypt gets directly from oil exports, oil revenues and trade have significant impact on Egyptian labour remittances, on the Suez Canal revenues, and, though to a lesser extent, on tourism. Already in 1976, Egypt was getting from oil exports more than double the value of cotton exports and more than the whole of its agricultural exports put together. Much of the total stock of private foreign investment in Egypt is in oil, the proportion of U.S. investment in the oil sector reaching as much as 82% of the total stock of U.S. investment at the end of 1991.[7] Although the share of oil revenues in total receipts of foreign exchange declined heavily in recent years, reaching only one-tenth in 1989/90 (Table 3.2), this was due more to the fall in oil revenues themselves than to the rise in other sources of revenue. Following the fall in oil prices in 1986, the flow of private foreign investment in Egypt declined by about one third.[8]

Like labour remittances, Egypt's revenues from oil exports have been little affected by domestic policy measures; the major determinant has been the development of international oil prices. In the face of fairly constant proven reserves of crude oil (see Table 3.8 below), production increase was restrained, and both production and export volume remained fairly stable since the big fall in oil prices in 1986, allowing revenues from oil exports to decline heavily (see Table 3.7).

Devaluation of the Egyptian pound is powerless as a policy instrument to increase oil revenues since it has no influence on the foreign currency value of oil. The main policy measure taken by the government to influence oil exports was the raising of domestic prices of petroleum products. Between 1986 and 1990 domestic energy prices were increased by more than 330% including tripling the price of fuel oil, the most heavily subsidized of petroleum products. In 1991, prices were raised again making the price to the consumer of butane

---

[7] U.S. Embassy in Cairo: *Foreign Economic Trends and Their Implications for the U.S., Report for the A.R.E.*, June, 1992.

[8] World Bank, *A.R.E.: Economic Readjustment with Growth*, Feb. 1990, vol. 2, p. 9.

TABLE 3.7
Annual Fluctuations in Egypt's Revenues
From Oil Exports
(1974–1989/90)

Year	Millions of U.S.$	% Change	Year	Millions of U.S.$	% Change
1974	187	–	82/83	2807	−16
1975	289	+54	83/84	2957	+5
1976	644	+12.3	84/85	2891	−2
1977	720	+12	85/86	2210	−24
1978	802	+11	86/87	1364	−38
1979	1880	+134	87/88	1532	+12
1980/81	3013	+60	88/89	1240	−19
1981/82	3329	+10	89/90	1229	−1

Source: 1974–80/81: World Bank: *A.R.E.: Issues of Trade Strategy and Investment Planning*, January 1983, p. 412; 1981/2–89/90: Table 3.1 above.

TABLE 3.8
Production, Domestic Consumption and
Proved Reserves of Petroleum
and Natural Gas
(1970–1990)

	Production (million tons)			Domestic Consumption (mill. tons)	Proved Reserves	
	Crude Petroleum	Natural Gas	Total		Crude Petroleum (billion barrels)	Natural Gas (trillion cubic feet)
1970	16.4	–	16.4	5.9	4.5	5000
1975	11.7	–	11.7	7.5	3.9	4000
1980	29.4	2.0	31.4	13.0	2.9	2970
1981	31.8	2.2	34.0	14.9	3.9	2960
1982	32.9	2.4	35.3	16.5	3.3	7180
1983	36.0	2.8	38.8	18.5	3.4	7100
1984	41.2	3.7	44.9	20.7	3.2	6996
1985	44.3	4.5	48.8	21.8	3.9	7067
1986	40.2	5.2	45.4	22.2	3.3	10247
1987	45.2	5.9	51.1	24.0	3.4	10247
1988	42.9	6.8	49.7	24.5	3.3	11484
1989	43.0	7.4	50.4	25.5	3.4	11700
1990	44.0	7.7	51.7	26.3	3.5	12400

Source: Abdallah, H.: *The Economics of Energy in Egypt*, Academy of Scientific Research and Technology, Cairo, 1992, (Arabic) pp. 164–5.

gas nearly four times what it was in 1985 and that of gasoline about 3.5 times higher. As a result, domestic consumption of some petroleum products showed very little increase and total domestic consumption showed remarkably lower rates of increase since 1985 than in the previous five years (see Table 3.9). These price increases have brought domestic prices much closer to international prices but, since they started from very low levels, the weighted average of energy prices in Egypt were still less than half of world prices in 1991. The Egyptian government has committed itself to reach the international levels of energy prices by 1995, which, according to a 1990 World Bank report, will require an average annual increase in domestic prices by as much as 35% until then. If this is achieved, the Bank estimates that this could increase Egypt's export earnings by about $1.5 billion per annum,[9] which is about equal to the total revenue from oil exports at present.

Egypt's hopes in raising its revenues from oil exports hinge upon four possible developments: (1) a rise in international oil prices, (2) discovering new oil fields, (3) further reduction in the consumption of petroleum products allowing more for export, and (4) the substitution of oil by natural gas, again allowing more of the former to be exported. The first two developments are difficult to predict and there are no strong reasons for optimism with regard to either of them. Petroleum officials in Egypt have expressed optimism about the production potential of the Western Desert, where the number of oil wells drilled is less than half those drilled in the Gulf of Suez, which has only one-tenth of the area of the Western Desert. The results of exploration there have not, however, supported this optimism. The early goal of producing one million barrels of oil a day by 1983 is not yet reached, since new discoveries have not added much to proved reserves.

With regard to rationalizing consumption of petroleum products, there have been estimates indicating the possibility of saving 27% of the power used in industry and 57% of residential consumption of fuel, but the five-year plan estimates of consumption during the plan years (92/3–96/7) are based on assuming an annual rate of growth of total domestic consumption of 2.9%[10] which is the same as the rate of the last four years (see Table 3.8 above). It is indeed difficult

---

[9] World Bank: *op.cit.*, pp. 32–3.

[10] *Middle East Economic Survey*, 3 February 1992, pp. A4 and A7.

TABLE 3.9
Domestic Consumption of Petroleum Products
and Natural Gas
(1952–1991)

(100 metric tons)

Year	Natural Gas	Butane Gas	Gasoline	Kerosene	Diesel	Fuel Oil	Asphalt and Other Products	Total	Rate of Change (%)
1952	–	4	252	665	343	1754	39	3057	–
1960	–	20	262	736	782	2783	158	4741	5.6
1965	–	59	287	928	1124	2974	209	5581	3.3
1970	–	108	444	820	1176	3005	366	5919	1.2
1975	33	179	656	1188	1335	3639	429	7459	4.7
1980	1616	382	1158	1503	2424	5172	787	13042	11.8
1981	1843	437	1275	1616	3008	5883	868	14930	14.5
1982	2035	476	1433	1782	3291	6548	945	16510	10.6
1983	2285	520	1610	1994	3720	7258	1144	18531	12.2
1984	3030	580	1809	2118	4147	7671	1383	20737	11.9
1985	3692	615	1958	2189	4058	7860	1459	21831	5.3
1986	4274	666	2025	2328	2875	7656	1390	22214	1.8
1987	4750	739	2105	2384	4058	4522	1450	24008	8.1
1988	5337	722	2109	2444	4173	8193	1500	24478	2.0
1989	5889	821	2141	2386	4347	8343	1546	25473	4.1
1990	6127	854	2172	2333	4515	8642	1655	26298	3.2
1991	6862	864	2095	2210	4634	8616	1643	26924	2.4

Source: Abdallah, H.: *The Economics of Energy in Egypt*, Academy of Scientific Research and Technology, Cairo, 1991, (Arabic), p. 165.

to see how this rate could be reduced much further. Several foreign advisers have stressed the possibility of substituting natural gas, of which Egypt has relatively large reserves (12 trillion cubic feet) for crude oil of which the current level of reserves officially estimated at 4 billion barrels, would be exhausted after 12 years at the current rate of production. The new five-year plan does not envisage, however, that such substitution would proceed during the plan years at a rate sufficiently great to make an impact on revenues from oil exports. In fact, this plan assumes a *decrease* in oil-export revenues, in real terms, at an annual rate of 4.7% (Table 3.6 above), with the aim, in the words of the plan "of gradually reducing the dependence on crude oil exports, preserving national wealth and protecting the plan from any shocks that could threaten its sources of finance, resulting from instability in the international oil prices".[11] Unless new and important oil discoveries are made, the fear of Egypt turning into a net importer of oil instead of a net exporter early in the next century, will continue.

3.4 *The Suez Canal*

The Suez Canal did not become part of the national economy until its nationalization in 1956, and did not start to bring net revenue to Egypt up to 1960. After eight years of closure following the 1967 war, its contribution to the balance of payments showed regular increase until in the late 1980's, with low oil prices, it surpassed the contribution of oil (Table 3.10).

Once Egypt had done the necessary work of widening and deepening the Canal, the Canal revenues became largely beyond Egypt's control. These revenues are governed by the volume of traffic which varies with conditions of world trade, particularly in oil, and of war and peace in the region, as well as by the level of toll rates. These rates which are fixed on the basis of the cargo-carrying capacity and the size and type of vessel crossing the Canal, are freely determined by the Suez Canal Authority but they are constrained by the opportunity cost of alternative routes. Thus, although the toll rates have been increased year after year, they were mainly used to alleviate the impact of fluctuations in traffic.

[11] *The Preliminary Framework of the Third Five-Year Plan, 1992/3–1996/7*, vol. I, (Arabic), p. 247.

Except in unusually unstable conditions, the transit tonnage passing through the Canal is relatively static (see Table 3.11) and hence its revenues have not shown the same degree of fluctuations as did oil revenues or labour remittances. Apart from the period of closure as a result of war conditions (1967–74), the rate of increase in the Canal revenues declined between 1982/3 and 1985/6 as a result of the slow-down in world trade and the decline in the rate of growth of oil production in the area. The Canal, however, has maintained a fairly stable share in total receipts of foreign exchange during the 1980's at about one-tenth (Table 3.2).

The contribution of the Suez Canal to the improvement in the balance of payments during the five-year plan (1992/3–1996/7) is

TABLE 3.10
Annual Fluctuations in Suez Canal Revenues
(1975–1989/90)

Year	Millions of U.S.$	% Change	Year	Millions of U.S.$	% Change
1975	85	–	1983/84	957	2
1976	311	266	1984/5	974	–8
1977	428	38	1985/6	897	15
1978	514	20	1986/7	1028	12
1979	589	15	1987/8	1148	10
1980/1	780	32	1988/9	1269	3
1981/2	909	16	1989/90	1300	13
1982/3	957	5		1472	

Source: 1974–1980/81: World Bank: *A.R.E.: Issues of Trade Strategy and Investment Planning*, January 1983, p. 412.
1981/82–1989/90: Table 3.1 above.
1990/91: Table 3.3 above.

TABLE 3.11
Suez Canal Traffic

Year	Number of Vessels	Passengers (thousands)	Net Tonnage (1000 tons)	Cargo (1000 ton)
1966	21250	0.3	274250	24
1985	19791	16	352579	25
1986	18403	12	366076	26
1987	17541	11	347038	25
1988	18190	14	306913	25
1989	17628	7	373429	26
1990	17664	7.5	410322	27

Source: CAPMAS: *Statistical Yearbook*, June 1991, p. 107.

therefore expected to be modest. Its share in the total fixed investment of the plan is only L.E. 500 million or 0.3% of total fixed investment,[12] and the rate of increase in its revenue during the five years is the moderate rate of 4.4% per annum (Table 3.6).

3.5 *Tourism*

Over the last fifteen years, Egypt's revenues from tourism have shown a distinctly rising trend. Between the mid and late 1970's, they rose from an average of $354 million (1974–76) to $677 million (1977–79), an increase of 91%, and by the late 1980's they have risen by another 40% (see Table 3.12). In recent years, tourism has been the brightest aspect of Egypt's balance of payments as well as the most dynamic source of foreign exchange. The figures in Table 3.12 are of receipts coming through the official market but if one is to add those obtained by the free market, particularly before the devaluation of 1987, the total would be much larger. In fact, estimates of the Ministry of Tourism, which includes both parts, are sometimes as much as five times those of the Central Bank.

This increase in income from tourism is perhaps less of the nature of "windfall incomes" than those from oil or the Suez Canal, since

TABLE 3.12
Annual Fluctuations in Foreign Exchange
Receipts from Tourism
(1974–1989/90)

Year	Million US $	% Change	Year	Million US $	% Change
1974	265	–	1982/3	304	–23
1975	332	25	1983/4	288	–5
1976	464	40	1984/5	410	42
1977	728	57	1985/6	315	–23
1978	702	–4	1986/7	380	21
1979	601	–14	1987/8	886	133
1980/1	712	18	1988/9	901	2
1981/2	393	–45	1989/90	1067	18

Sources: 1974–1980/81: World Bank: A.R.E.: *Issues of Trade Strategy and Investment Planning*, January 1983, p. 412.
1981/82–1989/90: Table 3.1 above.
1990/91: Table 3.3 above.

[12] *Preliminary Framework of the Third Five-Year Plan, op.cit.*, vol. 1, p. 177.

much of it is in return of increased investment. Over the last ten years, investment in the tourism sector has been growing considerably faster than in oil or in transport, communication and storage, which includes the Suez Canal (see Table 3.13).

There is still, however, wide scope for increasing tourist revenues and for government action to make this possible. An increase and versification of accommodation facilities are still required, as well as improvement in infrastructure especially in the relatively new areas along the Mediterranean and Red Sea coasts, expanding training institutions to satisfy the manpower needs of the tourism sector and upgrading the promotion efforts of the government and tourist agencies. With the exchange rates finally unified in October 1991, there is little scope for using the exchange rate as a policy instrument for increasing tourist receipts, and the main action required seems to be to increase investment in the various areas just mentioned. The new plan does not envisage any significant role for public investment in tourism up to 1997, but the private sector is assigned about the same proportion of total investment (3.0%)[13] as that fulfilled by both sectors during the last ten years (3.3%). This is planned to increase tourist revenues at an average annual rate of 10.9% during the plan years, which is the highest rate of increase envisaged in the plan other than that of manufacturing (Table 3.6 above). This may seem too optimistic but is in fact much lower than the rate of growth of tourist revenues in the five years preceding the plan (see Table 3.12).

The main problem with Egypt's revenues from tourism is neither the smallness of its contribution nor the lack of opportunities for its growth in the long and medium term, but rather its tendency for violent year-to-year fluctuations. In this respect, tourism is even a less reliable source of foreign exchange for Egypt than oil, the Suez Canal or labour remittances. Not only do tourist revenues tend to fluctuate with changes in world economic conditions but they are sensitive to political fluctuations, security threats in Egypt and in the whole region, as well as to changes in Egypt's political relationships especially with other Arab countries and Israel. These fluctuations seem to act more on tourism than on the other three sources of foreign exchange discussed in this chapter. Thus, the deterioration in Egypt-Arab relations following Sadat's visit to Jerusalem in 1977 and

[13] *Preliminary Framework*, *op.cit.*, p. 178.

TABLE 3.13
Investment in Selected Sectors (1982/3–1991/2)

(million L.E.)

Sector	82/3	83/4	84/5	85/6	86/7	87/8	88/90	89/90	90/1	91/2	Total	%
Agriculture	393.1	525.4	605.3	860.2	741.2	1552.2	1708.6	1865.8	1951.7	1992.0	12195.6	7.1
Manufacture & Mining	1726.3	2002.6	2387.1	3296.7	3962.4	4935.9	4811.9	5541.1	4838.2	5553.5	39055.7	22.7
Petroleum	1390.9	1429.3	1439.3	1459.8	1393.1	1696.5	2213.8	2487.0	3147.0	3147.0	20029.5	11.6
Electricity & Energy	548.0	572.0	1029.6	1156.1	700.8	3304.1	2314.1	2475.4	3434.2	1656.1	17190.4	10.0
Construction	226.4	263.7	166.1	217.6	234.9	295.1	351.6	395.9	438.0	446.5	3025.8	1.7
Transit, Communication Storage & Suez Canal	1897.2	1840.3	2049.8	2459.3	3100.0	3839.8	3132.0	3872.4	4208.0	3783.3	30182.0	17.5
Tourism	227.0	374.2	308.8	373.8	590.3	645.2	765.3	809.2	762.3	878.2	5734.3	3.3
Housing	799.3	924.8	1188.8	1565.8	1809.8	1677.7	2606.3	2446.6	2690.0	3041.0	18750.1	10.9
Public Utilities	358.2	509.1	662.2	772.2	960.5	1806.4	1627.4	1639.0	1679.0	1986.5	12000.5	7.0
Total Fixed Investment	8390.3	9150.9	10628.9	13014.4	14593.1	21091.2	20987.9	23450.8	25292.2	25106.8	171606.5	100.0

Source: Ministry of Planning: *Preliminary Framework of the Third Five-Year Plan (1991/2–96/7)* (Arabic), vol. 1, pp. 66 & 69.

the Camp David and Peace agreements of the following two years, were important factors behind the decline in tourist revenues in those years; political uncertainties following the assassination of President Sadat in 1981 and again the deterioration in the relationship between Egypt and the U.S. as well as the security problems in 1985/6 caused an even greater decline. Tourist revenues quickly revived after the Gulf crisis of 1990/91 but again suffered greatly from the terrorist actions of religious extremists in the winter of 92/93.

3.6 *The Rentier Economy and External Debt*

It is reasonable to presume that, other things equal, the more an economy relies on sources of income that are greatly influenced by factors outside the country's control, and are subject to violent and unpredictable fluctuations, the more this economy is likely to fall into debt. This is even more likely to be the case if these sources of income are interlinked and tend to move in the same direction. With wise economic management, a country may be able to avoid falling into debt if sufficient restraint is practised during relatively prosperous periods so as to meet the shortages of harsher times. If this is the case, the country could take advantage of rising external resources to repay old debts and invest in sufficiently productive projects to generate enough income that would make the country better equipped to face the decline in these resources. If the country is not so fortunate in the quality of economic management, it may find itself, once the sources of foreign exchange start to dwindle, forced to depend on borrowing from abroad.

Since the mid 1970's, Egyptian folly seems to have gone even further than this. We have already seen in Chapter One, how Egypt's long and medium-term civilian debt increased by as much as 76% in the four years 1977–81. These were the years in which all the four sources of income discussed in the present chapter (taken together) increased most rapidly, so that their share in the total current receipts of foreign exchange other than official transfers, rose from 55% in 1977 to 75% in 1981/2. Not only did Egypt fail to use this windfall increase in income to reduce the burden of external debt but it actually got itself more hopelessly in debt than ever. We have also seen how military debt also increased rapidly during the same period in spite of the fact that this very period witnessed the acceleration of peace efforts which culminated in the peace treaty of 1979.[14]

Rather than windfall incomes reducing the recourse to foreign borrowing, one may be tempted to ask whether the exact opposite may be nearer to the truth. In other words, it may not be the need to borrow that pushes the country into debt but rather the urge to lend, activated by the confidence in the borrower's ability to repay. Egypt's experience with foreign debt, both in the last century and in the present one, seems to support this view.

During the American civil war (1861–64), the output of American cotton dropped drastically leading to a sharp rise in the demand for Egyptian cotton, and about a 100% increase in its price during the first two years of the reign of the Egyptian Khedive, Ismail Pasha (1863–5). The volume of exports increased at about the same rate, so that the value of exports more than tripled during those two years.[15] But it was precisely those two prosperous years that witnessed the beginning of the infamous story of Egypt's external debt of the last century. Ismail had inherited some external debt from his predecessor, Said Pasha, but the burden of this debt was quite light, half of it being payable over 30 years, while the other short-term debt could have been repaid if government expenditure were to be reduced by about 20% during the first five years of Ismail's reign.[16] This was not done, however, as it was also not done during Sadat's reign a century later, when a similar effort could have relieved Egypt of the relatively small burden of debt of the 1960's and early 1970's. Instead, consumption habits under both Ismail and Sadat were radically transformed with an increasing tendency to satisfy the new consumption habits through importation. John Marlowe tells a fascinating story of both the pressure and the temptation to which Ismail was subjected from foreign banks, consuls and dealers of all kinds, to increase his purchases of goods, which were often of little use to the country, and of services that were often fictitious.[17] We have already seen what amounts to a very similar story of Sadat's expenditure and borrowing abroad especially in connection with his arms purchases. More important reasons for Ismail's extravagance than his

---

[14] See Chapter One.

[15] Crouchley, A.: *The Economic Development of Modern Egypt*, Longmans, London 1938, p. 134.

[16] This is based on figures of government revenues and expenses mentioned in Crouchly, *op.cit.*, p. 275.

[17] Marlowe, J.: *Spoiling the Egyptians*, Andre Deutsch, London 1974, pp. 111–125.

personal inclinations, may perhaps be found in the development of the balance-of-payment surplus of some European countries about the middle of the last century. There was clearly much more capital to lend in the 1860's than twenty years earlier.[18] Again, a similar interpretation could be offered for the increase in Sadat's expenditure and borrowing abroad following the big rise in oil revenues of 1973–4 and the accumulation of loanable funds in European and American banks. Egypt was by no means alone, neither in the 1860's and 1870's, nor in the 1970's, in getting itself unnecessarily into debt. During both periods, this was a widely spread phenomenon caused less by the irresponsible behaviour of this or that ruler than by pressure from outside. Egypt's bankruptcy in 1876 came one year after that of the Ottoman empire, and Egypt's debt crisis of the early 1980's was also part of a world-wide phenomenon. A Nigerian economist describes his country's experience in the 1970's in terms that fit Egypt very well:

> In 1978, when Nigeria agreed to contract the first billion of these debts, it had more income from oil than it could sensibly spend.... At first, to justify a relatively minor loan of $1 billion to be added to our huge oil revenues, we were encouraged to go on a spending spree. We were even helped to put together a lavish purchasing catalogue that we mistook for a development plan.[19]

It is just as ironic that the process of heavy borrowing abroad comes to an end, not when the need to borrow is weakened, but when it is most acute. When the flow of windfall incomes starts to dwindle, the country is urged to dispense with more borrowing and to give more attention to its more productive sectors. Much of this new attention to productive sectors is motivated by the need to repay the debt. In Egypt's earlier experience, the British occupation led to an intensive effort to develop and rationalize agricultural production, one of the main aims of which being to enable Egypt to repay its external debt.[20] In the more recent experience of the 1980's, the pressure

---

[18] See Landes, D.: *Bankers and Pashas*, Cambridge, Mass., 1958. See also Condliffe, J.: *The Commerce of Nations*, Norton, N.Y., 1950, p. 322.

[19] Chinweizu: "Debt Trap Peonage", *Monthly Review*, November 1985, pp. 23–4.

[20] According to Ali El-Gritly, "The sole aim of the British administration was the extension of perennial irrigation and the area under cotton with a view to providing

to pursue "structural adjustment" policies and the new urge towards export promotion, in both agriculture and manufacturing, could also be seen as a response to similar motives. The earlier experience, which lasted until the Second World War, did end with Egypt finally repaying the last of its debts in 1943, and with Egypt having more developed agriculture and manufacturing than when the British first came in 1882. But Egypt continued to have a lopsided economic structure which paved the way for falling again into debt.[21]

---

sufficient foreign exchange to meet the service of the large external debt" ("The Structure of Modern Industry in Egypt", *L'Egypte Contemporaine*, nos. 241–2, Nov.–Dec., 1947, p. 367). D. Mead comments on this by saying "whether or not this was the sole aim of British policy, it surely was a dominant one, see U.K. Foreign Office, Reports on the Finances, Administration and Condition of Egypt and the Progress of Reforms (London, H.M.S.O., May 1898) pp. 20–21 where the Earl of Cromer justifies government expenditure on the construction of a dam at Aswan in these terms." Mead, D.: *Growth and Structural Change in the Egyptian Economy*, Richard Irwin, Illinois, 1967, p. 7.

[21] It was remarked in the June symposium that there is nothing odd in a country being lent more in times of prosperity than when it is in need. Lenders are naturally influenced by the credit worthiness of the country which they consider lending to. Offers of loans may therefore increase when the country is least in need and demand for repayment as well as scarcity of loanable funds increase when the country's credit worthiness declines. This could explain Egypt's two experiences referred to in the text and there is therefore nothing ironical or unnatural about it as the text may imply. This may be so as long as purely economic factors are at work. What is suggested here, however, is that in the relationship between developed (lending) and underdeveloped (borrowing) countries, the relationship is governed by much more than market forces. In both experiences of Ismail Pasha and Sadat, various types of pressure were used to induce Egypt into unnecessary borrowing as well as wasteful uses of funds. The harshness of the measures used to extract repayment when times get harder seems therefore to be more cruel than it would have been had the borrowed funds been really needed and/or used more productively.

The same point may be made in connection with the lack of wise management of fluctuating incomes from the four sources of foreign exchange discussed in this chapter. I have mentioned in the text that heavy fluctuations in foreign exchange revenues are not necessarily damaging to development effort, if economic management is wise enough to control spending during periods of affluence so as to be able to face foreign exchange shortages in other periods. The same "non-economic" factors just referred to, may actually be the main reason why Egypt has more often than not been deprived of that kind of economic management.

CHAPTER FOUR

AGRICULTURE

4.1 *A Poor Performance*

The story of the mediocre performance of Egyptian agriculture over the last four decades is well known. The best period, as far as the rate of growth of output is concerned seems to have been that of the first five-year plan of 1959/60–1964/5, with an average annual growth rate of 3.3%,[1] growth rates being well below this rate before and after the plan years. During the 1950's, it was below 1%[2] and between the mid 1960's and mid 1970's less than 2%.[3] Since the mid 1970's, the annual rate of growth was above 2% but below the rate of population growth of 2.7% (see Tables 4.1 and 4.2 below). Growth of agricultural output has therefore been consistently below the growth of the economy as a whole, so that the share of agriculture in GDP showed a regular decline from 36% in 1952/3 to 25% in 1969/70[4] to 20% in 1981/2 to 17% in 1986/7 (see Table 4.2). The higher share of agriculture in GDP in the last few years is mainly a reflection of low oil prices, but the declining trend is continuing. The declining contribution of agriculture to the *growth* of output since the 1950's is shown in Table 4.3 from which it appears that the contribution of agriculture to growth during the 1980's was about half its contribution during the 1960's. Food production has shown a similarly poor performance so that per capita output of both food and total agriculture is lower now than it was forty years ago.

One of the few bright aspects of agricultural development since the mid 1970's has been the growth of fruit and vegetable production. Between the mid 1970's and mid 1980's production of citrus fruits increased by about 25%, other fruits by about a third, vegetables by

[1] Hansen, B.: "Planning and Economic Growth in the UAR (Egypt), 1960–5", in Vatikiotis, P.: *Egypt since the Revolution*, Allen and Unwin, London, 1968, p. 31.
[2] Ikram, *op.cit.*, p. 173.
[3] *ibid.*, pp. 172–3.
[4] Mabro, R.: *The Egyptian Economy*, Clarendon Press, Oxford, 1974, p. 189.

more than 40% and potatoes by more than 100%.[5] Otherwise the picture is rather grim.

Over the 12-year period between the early 1970's and mid 1980's maize, which is one of the principal crops occupying about one-sixth of all cropped area, realized some increase in yield and in cultivated area but several other major crops showed surprisingly little change, whether in yield per *feddan*, cultivated area or total production. This was true of wheat, rice, sugar cane and bersim, occupying together nearly half of the total cropped area, while cotton and millet, occupying together over one-tenth of the land, showed a distinct decline in cultivated area, fairly stable yield and hence a clear decline in total production.

4.2 *Trade Deficit*

This poor performance of agricultural production was reflected in a similarly poor performance of agricultural exports and a rapid growth of imports. In the mid 1980's, the value of cotton exports and that of total agricultural exports were respectively 10% and 14% less than ten years earlier, and the contribution of agriculture to total merchandise exports was one-third of what it was in the mid 1970's. Imports of wheat and flour increased by over 50% during those ten years, and other agricultural imports increased even faster, so that total agricultural imports in the mid 1980's were 140% higher than they were ten years earlier. Since other imports were also increasing rapidly, the share of agricultural imports in total imports remained at about one-fourth, but the share of deficit in the trade of agricultural goods to total balance of trade deficit doubled within a decade (see Table 4.4), and the rate of self-sufficiency declined heavily since 1960, as shown in Table 4.5.

4.3 *Alternative Explanations*

For almost twenty years now, the same explanation for the poor performance of Egyptian agriculture has been repeated over and over again and is persistently adhered to by the reports of international

[5] CAPMAS, *Statistical Yearbook*, June 1991, pp. 44–8, and World Bank: *U.A.R.: Issues of Trade Strategy*, 1983, p. 424.

TABLE 4.1
Changes in Agricultural Production (1971–80)

(million US$ at constant Prices)

	Average 1969–71	71	72	73	74	75	76	77	78	79	80
Value of Crops	1270.0	1296.0	1314.4	1307.5	1272.8	1287.9	1323.7	1274.7	1360.4	1428.9	1490.8
Value of Livestock	554.9	571.6	581.7	596.8	618.3	667.0	673.3	707.1	709.6	726.6	632.5
Total Agriculture	1824.9	1867.8	1896.1	1904.3	1891.1	1954.9	1997.0	1981.8	2070.0	2155.5	2223.3
% Change	–	2.4	1.5	0.4	–0.7	3.4	2.1	–0.8	4.4	4.1	3.2
Total Food	1475.7	1525.7	1550.8	1572.2	1592.4	1695.2	1728.1	1709.0	1771.0	1825.6	1862.7
% Change	–	3.4	1.7	1.3	1.3	6.5	1.9	–1.1	3.6	3.1	2.0
Per Capita Agricultural (69–71=100)	100	100	99	98	95	96	96	93	95	96	96
Per Capita Food (69–71=100)	100	101	100	100	99	103	102	99	100	101	100

Sources: J. Dethier: *Trade, Exchange Rate and Agricultural Pricing Policies in Egypt*, World Bank Comparative Studies, 1989, vol. 1, p. 19.

TABLE 4.2
Changes in Agricultural Production and its Share in Gross Domestic Product (1981/2–90/1)

	(a) 1981/2	(a) 82/3	(a) 83/4	(a) 84/5	(a) 85/6	(a) 86/7	(b) 87/8	(b) 88/9	(b) 89/90	(b) 90/1
Value of Agricultural Product (million L.E. at Constant Prices)	3932	4044	4131	4263	4353	4444	8640	8903	9141	9440
% Change	–	2.8	2.1	3.2	2.1	2.1	–	3.0	2.7	3.3
Total GDP at Factor Cost (million L.E. at Constant Prices)	20097	21585	22900	24411	25057	25689	40885	43069	45419	47911
Share of Agriculture in GDP (%)	19.6	18.7	18.0	17.5	17.4	17.3	21.1	20.7	20.1	19.7

(a) at constant 1981/2 prices
(b) at constant 86/7 prices
Sources: (1981/2–86/7: World Bank: *A.R.E.: Economic Readjustment with Growth*, 1990, vol. 3, p. 5.
1987/8–90/1: National Bank of Egypt: *Economic Bulletin*, 1991, No. 1–2, p. 104.

TABLE 4.3
Contribution of Agriculture to Growth of Output
(1945–82)

	1945 to 1952–3	1952–3 to 1959–60	1959–60 to 1964–5	1965–6 to 1970–1	1970–1 to 1974	1974 to 1981–2	1981/2 to 1986/7	1987/8 to 1990/1
Share of Agriculture in Growth of Output (%)	7.7	21.6	18.1	14.2	12.3	8.2	9.2	11.4

Sources: Hansen, B.: *The Political Economy of Poverty, Equity and Growth*: *Egypt and Turkey*, World Bank, 1991, p. 8, except for 1981–2 to 1986–7: and 1987/8 to 1990/1: Calculated from Table 4.2

TABLE 4.4
Exports and Imports of Agricultural Commodities

(million U.S.$)

	1974	75	76	77	78	79	80/1	81/2	82/3	83/4	84/5	85/6
Exports of Cotton	663	371	312	457	286	348	380	380	314	452	414	356
Other Agricultural Exports	194	155	231	260	223	198	260	190	159	211	140	119
Total Agricultural Exports	857	526	543	717	509	546	640	570	473	663	554	475
Total Merchandise Exports	1818	1875	2169	2346	2558	4024	6002	5779	5248	5924	6075	5193
% of Agricultural to Total Merchandise Exports	47	28	25	31	20	14	11	10	9	11	9	9
Imports of Wheat and Flour	798	642	547	600	841	772	1086	1130	834	1056	1013	983
Other Agricultural Imports	247	444	748	500	696	905	1470	1550	1559	1877	1698	1583
Total Agricultural Imports	1045	1086	1295	1100	1537	1677	2556	2680	2393	2933	2711	2566
Total Merchandise Imports	3618	4608	4659	5110	5993	7336	10039	10380	9619	11328	11593	10581
% of Agricultural to Total Merchandise Imports	29	24	28	21	26	23	25	26	25	26	23	24
Balance of Trade in Agricultural Commodities	−188	−560	−752	−383	−1028	−1131	−1916	−2110	−1920	−2270	−2157	−2091
Total Trade Balance	−1800	−2733	−2490	−2764	−3440	−3312	−4037	−4601	−4371	−5404	−5518	−5388
% of Deficit in Agri-Trade to Total Trade Deficit	10	20	30	14	30	34	47	46	44	42	39	39

Source: Taken or Calculated from: 1974–1980/1: World Bank: *Issues of Trade Strategy*, 1983, p. 412; 1981/2–1985/6: World Bank: *Economic Readjustment with Growth*, 1990, vol. 3, p. 10.

TABLE 4.5
Self Sufficiency in Major Food Items
(1960–1989)

	Wheat	Lentils	Maize	Sugar	Rice	Red Meat	White Meat	Dairy Products	Fish
1960	70	92	94	114	–	95	100	93	95
1965	35	93	93	99	137	81	–	–	–
1975	34	42	86	81	107	87	99	92	92
1980	25	10	77	57	75	75	65	62	54
1985	21	21	56	50	101	70	–	65	–
1989	26	17	76	64	103	66	–	–	–

Source: Commander, S.: *The State and Agricultural Development in Egypt Since 1973*, Ithaca Press, London, 1987, p. 38, except for 1985 and 1989, From Ministry of Supply: General Authority for Supply Commodities.

institutions. This explanation amounts, very briefly, to saying that the role of the state in Egyptian agriculture has been too pervasive. Official prices have been fixed by the state for a number of major crops, these prices usually being well below international prices, providing poor incentives for agricultural producers and resulting in a serious misallocation of resources. Subsidization of some major inputs, such as fertilizers and pesticides, have also sent contradictory price signals to farmers, aggravating resource misallocation. The whole of the cotton and sugarcane crops must be delivered to parastate agencies at the low officially-fixed prices together with a good portion of the rice crop. Other crops were also subject to the same system until October 1986, when the system was abandoned except for these three crops. Since then, all other crops have been allowed to be sold freely at prices determined by the free market. Subsidies for fertilizers and pesticides, though reduced, are still in operation, as well as subsidies given to some important food items, most importantly bread, which results in wasteful consumption. The artificially low profitability of some staples has led to an excessively high proportion of land being allocated to bersim, which has been made more profitable than other crops in which Egypt possesses greater comparative advantages. The profitability of bersim was also increased by the protection given to domestic meat production. All these forms of government intervention explain the slow growth of output of wheat and other crops, as well as the decline in the cotton area, output and exports.

This simple diagnosis leads to an equally simple recommendation: the dismantling of the system of administrative control of agricultural production and prices, liberalization of both domestic and international trade and the abandonment of state subsidies to food consumption and agricultural inputs.[6]

---

[6] There is hardly any need to refer the reader to the literature which adopts this diagnosis and makes this recommendation. Almost every single report on Egypt published by the World Bank or the IMF since the mid 1970's, including Khaled Ikram's book of 1980, as well as U.S. embassy reports, and the great majority of economic and other periodicals, both abroad and in Egypt, take the same stand. Bent Hansen's recent book comparing Egypt and Turkey, already referred to and also published by the World Bank, is less clearly committed to this view, especially that he notes that "heavily regulated Egyptian farmers seem thus to have done about as well as free-wheeling, largely unregulated Turkish farmers." (*The Political Economy of Poverty, Equity and Growth*, *op.cit.*, p. 475) But Professor Hansen tends to look at the whole period since 1960 as a homogenous one, without finding it necessary to distinguish between the better performance of the early period of state control and the

It is remarkable how this view emphasizes the disincentive to private investment in agriculture to the almost complete neglect of the role played by the decline in the share of agriculture in public investment which has continued to have the predominant share of total agricultural investment. Through the 1960's and 1970's, public investment constituted nearly 94% of total investment in agriculture,[7] but after 1965, the state has been allocating a rapidly decreasing share of its total investment to agriculture. After a rise in this share from 12–13% in the 1950's to over 23% during the years of the first five-year plan (1960–65), it fell to 20.4% for the rest of the decade. By 1975/6 it had fallen to around 8% of total investment and by 1980/1 to no more than 5.3%.[8] This share rose during the following decade (1982/3–1991/2) to 6.7%[9] but was still less than a third of what it was in the 1960's. Economic policy in the 1960's has sometimes been criticized for its relative neglect of agriculture in favour of industrialization, but the situation seems to have developed into one of "absolute" neglect during the following two decades. Drainage, irrigation and land reclamation have all suffered from the diversion of public investment elsewhere and agricultural extension services have almost ceased.

This decline in the share of agriculture in public investment has, of course, little to do with the relative profitability of various crops or with government intervention in agricultural prices and output. These considerations cannot also be the explanation of the relatively low share of agriculture in the allocation of foreign economic assistance to Egypt. This has indeed been a feature of American and other Western aid, as well as that coming from Arab states and the World Bank. Tables 4.6 and 4.7 show that agriculture (including food storage projects) absorbed no more than 6% of total U.S. project aid commitments to Egypt between 1975 and 1986, and only 17% of all loans extended by the World Bank and IDA to Egypt up to the end of 1989.[10]

later period following the launching of the open-door policy in the mid 1970's, during which state control in some areas was mixed with great laxity in others.

[7] Commander, S.: *The State and Agricultural Development in Egypt since 1973, op.cit.*, p. 35.

[8] Commander, *op.cit.*, pp. 22 and 35.

[9] Ministry of Planning: *Preliminary Framework of the Third Five-Year Plan*, vol. I, *op.cit.*, p. 64.

[10] It was objected in the June symposium that foreign aid should not be blamed for not going in large amounts to any particular sector, so long as it goes to areas where funds are needed. Once this condition is fulfilled foreign aid would always

TABLE 4.6
Distribution of U.S. Project Aid Commitments
To Egypt, by Sector (1975–86)

Sector	Project	$ million
Infrastructure:		*2415*
Electricity	Two power plants	513
	High Dam turbines rehabilitation	100
	Power plant equipment	132
	Urban power distribution equipment	127
	Natural Energy Control Center	43
Water & Sewage	Cairo sewage system	551
	Alexandria sewage	213
	Cairo water system	97
	Canal cities water & sewage	169
Telecommunications	Telephone system	247
Transport and Storage:	Grain silos & other food storages	161
	Port development & equipment	61
Productive Services		*863*
Industry	Cement plants	205
	Public sector loans	143
	Textile plant rehabilitation	91
	Private sector loans	200
Agriculture	Loans to farmers	84
	Agriculture & poultry development	29
	Agricultural mechanization	39
	Agriculture cooperative development	5
Irrigation	Canal maintenance and irrigation pumps	49
	Covered drainage	19
Decentralization		*796*
Social services		*396*
	Health & population control	231
	Education	165
Research and Technical Assistance:		*615*

Source: Handoussa, H.: *15 Years of U.S. Aid to Egypt*, a paper submitted to the 13th annual symposium, Center for Contemporary Arab Studies, Georgetown University, April 14–15, 1988, (mimeo.) pp. 54–5.

allow the government to go into the "neglected" sectors by relieving the government from investing in another important sector. This is, of course, true, but we are not here pronouncing judgement on foreign aid but trying to explain why Egyptian agriculture has performed so poorly.

TABLE 4.7
Loans from World Bank and IDA
To Egypt up to 31/12/1989)

Sector	$ million	Sector	$ million
Agriculture	538.7	Industry	610.3
Education	87.8	Telecommunications	64.0
Electricity	381.0	Transport	481.5
Energy	190.0	Urban Development	59.0
Energy Projects	13.5	Other	105.0
Water & Sewage Network	96.0		
Industrial Development & Finance	465.0	Total	3091.8

Source: World Bank.

Agriculture has also not been a very much favoured sector by private investment. During the 1980's, it received no more than 7.6% of total private investment, not much more than tourism (7.1%) and considerably below the share of housing (24.1%) (see Table 4.8), while private foreign investment has shown clear preference for oil,[11] and among the non-oil sectors, very low priority was given to agriculture (see Table 4.9). But private investment in agriculture, whether national or foreign, is, of course, not merely a function of how remunerative agriculture is but of how profitable it is compared with other sectors. Whether the role of the state in agriculture is pervasive or not, and hence, whether agriculture is a remunerative activity or not, may not be as decisive a determinant of private investment as what is happening in other sectors. Since the launching of the open-door policy in the mid 1970's, the relaxation of state control of other types of investment (not all of them legal), has made investment in agriculture relatively unattractive, with or without strict government control of agricultural prices and output. In fact, several aspects of government intervention in agriculture, though continuing to be nominally in force, were becoming easily evaded in practice.

The relative attractiveness of other sectors, such as housing, trade and tourism as well as certain types of manufacturing, have not only deprived agriculture of investment funds but has harmed agricultural

[11] Up to the end of 1988, the total stock of U.S. direct investment in Egypt had not exceeded $1.7 billion of which no less than 82% was in the oil sector. American Embassy in Cairo, *Egyptian Economic Trends*, March 1990, p. 17.

TABLE 4.8
Distribution of Private Fixed Investment by Sector
(1982/83–1991/92)

Sector	1982/3–1986/7 (L.E. Mil.)	1987/8–1991/2 (L.E. Mil.)	1982/3–1991/2 (L.E. million)	%
Agriculture	960	4481	5441	7.6
Manufacturing & Mining	5100	12550	17650	24.8
Petroleum	5637	11484	17121	24.1
Electricity & Energy	41	–	41	.1
Construction	368	872	1240	1.7
Total Commodity Sector	12106	29387	41493	58.3
Transport, Communications & Storage	1737	2458	4195	5.9
Trade, Finance & Insurance	764	1479	2243	3.1
Tourism	1619	3425	5044	7.1
Total Productive Services	4120	7362	11482	16.1
Housing	5266	11879	17145	24.1
Education	116	185	301	.4
Health	142	252	394	.6
Other Services	96	141	237	.3
Total Social Services	5620	12457	18077	25.4
Grand Total	21846	29206	71052	100

Source: Ministry of Planning: *Preliminary Framework of the Third Five-Year Plan, 1992/3–96/7*, (Arabic) vol. I, p. 65.

production in a more positive way. Encroachment on agricultural land by urban expansion and all types of construction has led to an estimated loss of 50,000 acres a year since the early 1970's. This implies a loss of about .45% of total cultivated area every year.[12] To this should be added the removal of the precious layers of the soil for use in the increasingly profitable brick factories. Laws which have been promulgated to prohibit both urban encroachment on agricultural land and the manufacturing of mud-bricks have been, until quite recently, rarely enforced. Rather than suffering from too much state

[12] Commander, *op.cit.*, p. 35.

TABLE 4.9
Sectoral Distribution of Operating Projects inside Egypt under Law 43

Year	Percent of Total Capital in Financial Projects	Percent of Total Non-Finance Capital				Percent of Total Investment In Financial Projects	Percent of Total Non-Finance Investment Costs			
		Indus-trial	Agricul-tural	Construc-tion	Services		Indus-trial	Agricul-tural	Construc-tion	Services
1976	76.4	50.0	0.0	5.1	44.9	–	–	–	–	–
1981*	58.9	51.3	15.6	11.0	22.1	41.9	43.4	17.3	17.9	21.4
1982	55.0	43.6	15.2	10.7	30.6	37.7	39.8	14.7	13.7	31.8
1984*	52.9	50.0	12.7	9.5	27.7	36.0	48.6	12.8	12.2	26.4
1985	48.9	53.0	9.0	11.7	26.3	30.0	55.1	8.2	11.4	25.2
1986	47.2	53.3	9.5	10.3	27.0	28.7	55.1	8.8	10.2	25.9
1987	45.7	54.2	8.9	10.1	25.8	27.7	55.7	8.4	10.0	25.9
1989*	37.9	54.7	8.8	12.2	24.3	22.3	57.5	8.4	11.5	22.6

Source: Esfahani, H.: *The Experience of Foreign Investment in Egypt under Infitah*, Faculty Working Paper, College of Commerce and Business Administration, University of Illinois at Urbana, Dec. 1990.
* mid-year values.

control, agriculture could have done quite well with a stricter enforcement of certain laws and with greater public investment in agricultural infrastructure. Whether a better allocation of resources resulting from the abandonment of government interference in the free play of market forces, would necessarily more than compensate for lower investment in agriculture resulting from the greater profitability of other sectors and for the loss of output resulting from urban encroachment and soil erosion, is far from obvious.[13]

4.4 *Agricultural Policy and Trade Deficit*

Nor is it obvious that the dismantling of state control is a sufficient guarantee for eliminating the agricultural trade deficit. Even if a liberalization policy does succeed in raising total agricultural output, the resulting composition of output may lead to less rather than greater self-sufficiency in agricultural products. The end result will, of course, depend on the structure of agricultural prices and the pattern of demand for both domestic products and imports. Both of these are greatly influenced by the pattern of income distribution and the degree of liberalization of imports. Those who advocate dismantling government control of agricultural output and prices also advocate import liberalization and are not sympathetic to the goal of self-sufficiency. They are usually also more tolerant of income inequalities. The whole policy package seems to be more conducive to more rather than less trade deficit in agricultural and food products. Indeed, it is very likely that the growing food and agricultural deficit of the last two decades was at least as much due to greater import liberalization and to

[13] One participant in the June symposium said that advocates of structural adjustment do not deny that the government should interfere in some areas. Of course, the government will continue to carry certain important responsibilities in agriculture as elsewhere, even under a program of "structural adjustment". The trouble is that the Egyptian government seems to have interfered where it should not have done, and abstained from interfering where it should have interfered. This may be a sound conclusion to the debate but it is still worth pointing out that in the literature advocating structural adjustment, such a balanced view is rarely if ever to be found. The responsibility of the decline in government activity for the poor performance of Egyptian agriculture is hardly ever mentioned in this literature, as well as the responsibility of other sectors being more profitable than agriculture, not always as a result of purely economic forces. Moreover, certain kinds of government action is categorically rejected in this literature, such as land reclamation, where the withdrawal may not be justified. Deliberate policies for achieving a minimum degree of self sufficiency, which are discussed later in this chapter, are also rejected.

changes in the pattern of demand resulting, partly, from the changing pattern of income distribution, as to excessive state control of agriculture.

To give one example, the persistently high share of bersim in total cultivated area is not merely the result of the low official prices of other competing crops, such as wheat, and of the protection of domestic meat production, but may also be to a large extent, the result of the pattern of income distribution maintaining a high level of demand for red meat. With the richest quarter of the population consuming about four times as much meat, poultry and eggs as the poorest quarter, the pattern of income distribution must have a strong impact on the rate of growth of demand, production and imports of livestock products. This may be an important reason why livestock production grew twice as fast as crop production between 1970 and 1980, and why the use of grains as animal feed grew much faster than for human consumption.[14] Changes in income distribution could thus be just as responsible for crop composition and the growth of demand and imports as government intervention in the level of output and prices. With unrestrained growth of income inequalities and without pursuing greater self-sufficiency as a deliberate goal of agricultural policy, there is no reason why the deficit in the international trade in agricultural goods should not grow as rapidly as before, with or without dismantling state control of agriculture.

The new five-year plan (1992/3–1996/7) aims at increasing agricultural output at an average annual rate of 3.5% which may not be unrealistic, but its goals regarding agricultural trade seem to be unduly optimistic. The planned rate of increase of agricultural exports of 9.5% annually is not in line with past performance and no significant reallocation of land between various crops is envisaged to make this possible. We have already seen how agricultural exports have declined rapidly after the mid 1970's (see Table 4.4 above) and even in recent years, after some liberalization of agricultural prices, the declining trend continued. In 1988/9–1989/90, the value of agricultural exports was about two-thirds of what it was 15 years earlier.[15] The plan does not have separate figures for agricultural

[14] See Mitchell, T.: "America's Egypt: Discourse of the Development Industry", *Middle East Report*, March–April 1991, pp. 21–22.

[15] Central Bank of Egypt: *Annual Report*, 1990/91, p. 185 and with Table 4.6 above.

imports, but the planned rate of increase for total imports of consumer goods (.9%) seems far too low in the light of past experience. Imports of agricultural goods have more than doubled between the mid 1970's and mid 1980's (see Table 4.4 above). There has indeed been a significant decline in the value of imports of some major food products in the last few years,[16] mainly of wheat and flour. Although this is partly a reflection of a significant rise in wheat production, it was also a result of a fall in the price of imports of wheat and flour as well as an increase in food aid associated with the Gulf War.

4.5 *An Import-Substitution Strategy for Agriculture*

About ten years ago, Dr. Moustafa Al-Gabaly, a distinguished agriculturist and an ex-minister of agriculture, put forward a detailed strategy for agricultural development in Egypt based not on faith in the benevolence of free market forces, but on the belief that planning and active state intervention were necessary to achieve the twin aims of higher self-sufficiency in basic food products and an adequate level of food consumption. The strategy is obviously relevant if one of our goals is also to minimize the need for external borrowing.

Al-Gabaly's proposed strategy[17] calls for action on five fronts: raising yields of major food crops, changing the structure of agricultural output, crop intensification, land reclamation and institutional changes. According to Al-Gabaly, there is still wide scope for significant increases in yields of such important crops as maize, wheat and rice with regard to which the "Green Revolution" has barely touched the Egyptian countryside. The introduction of high-yield varieties could increase the yield per *feddan* of maize from 11 to 27 *ardeb*s (a result actually achieved by successful experiments in some of the Delta provinces), the yield of wheat from 9–10 to 20 *ardeb*s and that of rice by about 60%. This alone could bring Egypt to almost a 100% self-sufficiency in maize, to dispense with about 25% of the imports of wheat and flour and to cover the expected increase in the consumption of rice over a decade.

[16] *ibid.*, p. 186.

[17] Al-Gabaly, M.: "The Road to Agricultural Development", *L'Égypte Contemporaine*, April 1981, pp. 89–101 (Arabic). See also his: *A Modern Look at Agriculture in Egypt*, Dar Al-Taawon, (Arabic) Cairo 1984, pp. 240–310.

The suggested change in crop composition consists mainly of reducing the land allotted to bersim and other fodder crops, which now occupies more than a fourth of the total cropped area, to about half its present area. This would save about 1.4 million *feddan* which could be allotted to some basic food crops as follows: 500,000 *feddan*s for the cultivation of sugarbeet, 150,000 for lentils, 150,000 for beans and 600,000 for winter crops that produce edible oil. The reduction in area under bersim would imply a reduction of the number of cattle by as much as 60%. The loss in meat and milk production is not as great, however, since a good part of the farm animals in Egypt consists of draft animals which have very low productivity of milk and meat. That part of the cattle which is dispensed with, could be replaced by much more productive varieties with a much higher transformation rate. Al-Gabaly estimates that such a change in crop composition could allow for a doubling of the output of milk, the improvement of the Egyptian diet by increasing the consumption of lentils and beans, which are the main sources in Egypt of vegetable protein and, through the increase in the area under sugarbeet, the dispensing with sugar imports for more than ten years.

The policy of crop intensification should aim at raising crop intensity to 300%, instead of the present 200% (i.e. increasing the number of crops from two to three per year), thus increasing the cropped area by about 50% to 16.5 million *feddan*s. These additional 5.5 million *feddan*s could be allocated to wheat (one million *feddans*, adding 1.8 million tons to our wheat production), maize (1.3 million *feddan*s which, together with the increase in yields already referred to, would allow a big increase in poultry and egg production), rice (one million *feddans*) as well as sugarbeet, edible-oil crops, such as peanuts, soya beans and sunflower, and a variety of vegetables.

Altogether, the results of increasing yields, changing crop composition and crop intensification would imply complete self-sufficiency in maize, sugar, lentils, beans and edible oil, poultry and eggs, a greater surplus of rice and vegetables and a 60% self-sufficiency rate in wheat.

In order to keep the land/population ratio constant, four million new acres of land are needed by the year 2000 over what existed in 1981, when Al-Gabaly's plan was put forward. A whole decade has passed since then and less than a fourth of this increase in cultivated area has been achieved. Now our time horizon has to be pushed beyond the year 2000 and greater effort is needed if the land/population ratio is not to fall much further. The main constraint to land reclamation is water. Assuming that the new land will produce only two crops a year and that every crop needs 3000 cubic meters of water, the total water requirements of the new 4 million acres are 24 billion cubic meters. To this must be added the expected increase in demand for water for industrial and household consumption. This was estimated at 13 billion cubic meters by the year 2000. If to these, one adds about 50 billion cubic meters needed for the existing land after crop intensification (16.5 million x 3000 cubic meters) the total water requirements would come to at least 87 billion cubic meters. These may be met, in addition to the roughly 55.5 billion available at present, by the water made available by the Jongly Canal (2 billion), other projects in the upper Nile (9 billion), whatever could be saved from the drainage water lost to the sea as a result of over-irrigation (12 billion), underground sources of water (5 billion), the rationalization of household consumption (1.5 billion) and recycling of water in industry (2 billion).[18] If all this materializes, Egypt will have increased its cropped area from about ll million to about 24.5 million acres (8 million from newly-reclaimed land and 16.5 from the land which already exists, after crop intensification).

It hardly needs mentioning that if all this is to be attempted, major institutional changes will be required in terms of wide national campaigns for spreading new practices among farmers, rationalizing the use of water (including charging a price for its use), government intervention in crop rotation and widespread mechanization to replace the displaced animals, which in turn would require great efforts in crop consolidation. The price to be paid in terms of a more pervasive role for the state may be considered too high to pay, but this may be a necessary condition for achieving a reasonable degree of self sufficiency in major food products.[19]

---

[18] These figures on water resources and requirements are from a lecture by Dr. Al-Gabaly given at the Egyptian Economic Society in January 1982. See also his *A Modern Look at Agriculture in Egypt*, *op.cit.*, pp. 300–307.

[19] Dr. Al-Gabaly's work, while highly praised, was nevertheless criticized in the June symposium for not sufficiently recognizing the practical difficulties involved in putting such a blue print into practice and for glossing over the discussion of how in fact to bring it into effect. One participant said that while she does not object to Dr. Al-Gabaly's scheme and accepts his goals, the actual implementation should be brought about through a system of "indicative planning" and without direct administrative control. Market forces and private incentives should be the means through which this goal be achieved. Perhaps, once the goal of a minimum self-sufficiency is adhered to, implementation would require a mixture of direct

administrative control, of the type practised in Egypt during the first five-year plan (1960–65) and what is called indicative planning. When adequate private response could be expected, there is no reason why compulsion should be used. The trouble, however, is that advocates of the so called "structural adjustment" reject both administrative intervention of almost any kind as well as the very goal of minimum degree of self-sufficiency. In both respects, Dr. Al-Gabaly's position is in direct opposition to this program. Although this structural adjustment program is likely to increase the rate of growth of agricultural output, it is far from obvious that it will reduce the deficit in the balance of trade in agricultural goods. A decline in both the rate of self-sufficiency in basic foodstuffs and in the quality of diet for a good proportion of the population is also likely to occur.

CHAPTER FIVE

MANUFACTURING INDUSTRY

5.1 *Disappointing Performance*

For some seventy years now, the diversification of the Egyptian economy through industrialization has been one of the main declared goals of official policy as well as of the Egyptian nationalist movement. The establishment of Bank Misr in 1920 continued to be glorified because of its commitment to industrial development, and the 1952 revolution considered rapid industrialization to be one of its main goals. Both were conscious reactions against excessive reliance on agriculture as a source of income and on cotton as a source of foreign exchange. Looking back at actual achievements, the judgement must be one of disappointment with the performance of manufacturing industry with respect to the diversification of both output and exports.

Thirty years after the establishment of Bank Misr, the share of manufacturing industry in GDP was still no more than 13%, and after another forty years it was only 18%. Comparing the rates of growth of industry with other sectors, industry does not seem to have been the engine of growth or the source of dynamism in the economy at any period since the fall of Mohamed Ali in the middle of the last century. Over the last fifty years, as Table 5.1 shows, there was no period during which the growth of industry (excluding petroleum) contributed more than one-third of the growth of GDP and, with the exception of the 1960's, in which industry contributed about one-third of total GDP growth, its contribution was less than a fourth.

The best period since the 1952 revolution with regard to the rate of growth of industry was undoubtedly that of the first five-year plan (1959/60–1964/5) when this rate reached 8.5%.[1] This rate has never been reached since then, with the rate of industrial growth, excluding petroleum which became important after 1974, ranging between

[1] Hansen, B.: "Planning and Economic Growth in the UAR 1960–5", in Vatikiotis, P. (ed.): *Egypt since the Revolution*, Allen and Unwin, London, 1968, p. 31.

TABLE 5.1
Contribution of Various Sectors to GDP Growth
(1945–1990/91)

Sector	1945 to 1952/3	1952/3 to 1959/60	1959/60 to 1964/65	1965/66 to 1970/71	1970/71 to 1974	1974 to 1981/2	1981/82 to 1986/87	1986/87 to 1990/91
Agriculture	0.3	0.8	1.0	0.4	0.4	0.7	.5	.7
Industry	0.7(a,b)	1.0(a,b)	1.8(a)	1.0(a)	0.3(a)	1.3(c)	.8(c)	1.3(c)
Other	3.5	2.0	2.8	1.7	2.7	6.9	4.3	3.7
Total GDP	4.5	3.8	5.6	3.1	3.4	8.9	5.6(d)	5.7(d)

(a) includes petroleum, which was unimportant before 1974
(b) includes electricity and public utilities
(c) manufacturing and mining (other than petroleum) only.
(d) for these two periods the Ministry of Planning's figures recorded here are significantly different from World Bank estimates.

Sources: 1945–1981/82: Hansen B. *The Political Economy of Poverty, Equity and Growth*, *op.cit.*, p. 16.
1981/82–1986/87: Calculated from World Bank: *A.R.E Economic Readjustment with Growth*, *op.cit.* vol. 3, p. 5.
1986/87–1990/91: Calculated from National Bank of Egypt: *Economic Bulletin*, 1991, No. 1, 2, p. 104.

TABLE 5.2
Growth of Output of Manufacturing Industry (1)

Year	Millions of Egyptian Pounds in Constant 1975 prices	% Change	Year	Millions of Egyptian Pounds in Constant 81/82 Prices	% Change	Year	Millions of Egyptian Pounds in Constant 86/87 Prices	% Change
1974	825	–	1981/82	2670	–	1986/7	6933	–
1975	880	6.7	82/3	2841	6.4	87/8	7453	7.5
1976	948	7.7	83/4	3071	8.1	88/9	7986	7.1
1977	1012	6.7	84/5	3270	6.5	89/90	8564	7.2
1978	1068	5.5	85/6	3384	3.5	90/91	9054	5.7
1979	1152	7.9	86/7	3456	2.1			
1980/81	1307	13.4						

(1) Including mining other than petroleum and its products.
Sources: 1974–1980/81: World Bank: *A.R.E.: Issues of Trade Strategy and Investment Planning*, January 14, 1985, p. 409.
1981/82–1986/87: World Bank: *A.R.E.: Economic Readjustment with Growth*, February 2, 1990, (vol. 3), p. 5.
1986/87–1990/91: National Bank of Egypt: *Economic Bulletin*, 1991, No. 1–2, p. 104.

6% and 8% (see Table 5.2). Thus after a rise in the share of manufacturing in GDP from 13% in 1952/3 to 18% (1955/6), 20% (1959/60), 22% (1964/5) and to 24% in 1969/70, it went into decline until it reached 18% in 1986/7 where it has stayed ever since.[2]

The share of manufacturing in exports has shown a similar pattern. Starting from 9% of total merchandise exports in 1950, this share showed a regular increase until 1974 when it reached 39%, but declined since then until the big fall in the price of oil in 1986 drove the share of manufactures up again (see Tables 5.3 and 5.4). The role which was played by cotton for 150 years has been taken over since the mid 1970's, not by manufactures but by oil. Exports of textiles, which have continued to dominate Egypt's manufactured exports, have been strikingly stagnant up to the late 1980's, and other manufactured exports did not do much better, so that the value of total manufactured exports in 1984/5–1985/6 were considerably smaller, in real terms, than it was ten years earlier. There seems to be a change for the better in the last few years but it is still too early to judge how lasting this will prove to be.

TABLE 5.3
Share of Industrial Exports in
Total Merchandise Exports (1950–70)

Year	%	Year	%
1950	9	1965	32
1955	14	1970	36
1960	20		

Source: Hansen, B.: *The Political Economy of Poverty* . . . pp. 138–9.

5.2. *Diagnosis and Prescriptions According to Conventional Wisdom*

As it is with agriculture, there are widely accepted diagnosis of the disease and prescriptions for treatment of Egyptian industry. This constitutes the conventional wisdom of the day and is endlessly repeated in academic, official, World Bank and IMF literature on the Egyptian economy. Very briefly, it boils down to saying little more than that Egyptian industry has been doing badly because it is largely

[2] ibid, p. 22; and Hansen, B.: *The Political Economy of Poverty, Equity and Growth*, p. 525, Ikram, L.: *Egypt: Economic Management in a Period of Transition*, pp. 400–401, and National Bank of Egypt: *Economic Bulletin*, 1991, no. 1–2, p. 104.

TABLE 5.4
Exports of Manufactures

(in millions of US$)

	1974	75	76	77	78	79	1980/1	81/2	82/3	83/4	84/5	85/6	88/9	89/90
Exports of Textile	366	478	301	300	272	267	370	280	199	265	294	288	446	635
Other Manufactured Exports(1)	344	398	497	317	515	351	550	260	411	463	444	436	531	667
Total Manufactured Exports(1)	710	876	798	617	787	618	920	540	610	728	738	724	977	1302
Total Merchandise Exports	1818	1875	2169	2346	2558	4024	6002	5779	5248	5926	6075	5193	2697	3145
% of Manufactures to Total Merchandise Exports %	39	47	37	26	31	15	15	9	12	12	12	14	36	41

(1) Not including petroleum products.

Sources: 1974–1980/1: World Bank: *Issues of Trade Strategy*, *op.cit.*, p. 412
1981/2–1985/6: World Bank: *Economic Readjustment with Growth*, *op.cit.*, vol. 3, p. 10.
1988/9–1989/90: Central Bank of Egypt: *Annual Report*, 2990/91, p. 185.

publicly owned, subject to excessive administrative control and inward looking. The solutions lie in privatization, dismantling the system of state control and replacing the import-substitution strategy by one of export promotion.

A relatively early exposition of what came to be conventional wisdom was made by a World Bank mission which visited Egypt in 1976–77 and published its report in 1980 in a widely circulated book.[3] According to this book, the performance of Egyptian industry began to deteriorate around 1963–4 mainly as a result of maladministration of the public sector. Under this wide term "maladministration" comes many causes of inefficiency such as growing bureaucracy, inefficient management, wastage of imports and raw materials, lack of maintenance, lack of incentives, inadequate supervision, negligence on the part of labour, etc.[4] In addition to maladministration, the blame is also directed to the import-substitution strategy according to which protection was extended to non-competitive industries such as iron and steel and car assembly. Administrative interference with international trade since the mid 1950's also led Egyptian trade to be directed to the Eastern bloc as a result of which Egypt "missed the advantages of exposure to the demanding requirements of quality and standardization of production in Western markets. Such an exposure might have spurred improvements in method of production and in efficiency."[5] The suggested solutions are mainly to expose industrial firms to the forces of competition, to overhaul industrial price policy to free it from administrative control and to remove price distortions, to provide greater incentives to exports, to reduce bureaucratic control on exports, and to introduce a more favourable exchange rate.[6]

It is interesting to note that at the time of this early World Bank mission, privatization had not yet become as fashionable as it is at present, hence the book does not put forward any suggestion with regard to public ownership but only suggests subjecting public sector management to market forces and giving it greater freedom over pricing decisions, employment, wages and maintenance.[7] The call for

---

[3] Ikram, K.: *Egypt: Economic Management in a Period of Transition*, published for the World Bank by Johns Hopkins University Press, Baltimore, 1980.

[4] *ibid.*, pp. 256–7.

[5] *ibid.*, p. 260.

[6] *ibid.*, pp. 264–7.

[7] *ibid.*, p. 270.

abandoning public ownership was to be made more explicit gradually so that by 1991, a report of the U.S. embassy in Cairo stated that "extensive state ownership in the industrial sector has burdened the economy and state budget with a variety of inefficient and overstaffed enterprises; large subsidies and pervasive economic controls, many designed to protect the public sector from competition, have encouraged waste, distorted resource flows and stifled productive incentives."[8]

Several prominent Egyptian economists have expressed the same view,[9] but perhaps the most eloquent and persistent Egyptian spokesman of this stand is Dr. Said El-Naggar, an ex-professor of Economics at Cairo University and a former executive director of the World Bank. In addition to numerous academic as well as popular articles published over the last ten years, he recently published an influential book[10] expanding his views on Egypt's major economic problems. In these writings, Dr. El-Naggar goes further than any other advocate of privatization, liberalization and than any critic of the public sector, import substitution and economic planning. To the predominance of the public sector he attributes the stagnation of exports, since it is responsible for about 80% of total merchandise exports, the high rate of unemployment, since it realizes 70% of all investments, and the large external debt, since about $20 billion of this debt consists of loans to public enterprises.[11]

More recently, Alan Roe, of the University of Warwick, presented a paper to a Cairo University conference in which he attributed the low productivity in Egyptian industry mainly to inward-looking and protectionist policies which he labels the "disorderly approach".[12] Four reasons are given for the adverse consequences of this approach for

[8] U.S. Embassy in Cairo: Foreign Economic Trends and their Implications for the U.S., Report for the A.R.E., April 1991, p. 3.

[9] See in particular: Handoussa, H.: "Reforms Policies for Egypt's Manufacturing Sector", in Handoussa, H. and Potter, G.: *Employment and Structural Adjustment: Egypt in the 1990's*, A.U.C. Press, Cairo, 1991, pp. 106–122; El-Beblawy, H.: *Change for the Sake of Stability* (Arabic), Dar Ul-Shorouq, Cairo, 1992, pp. 73–82 and Shehata, I.: *Programme for Tomorrow*, (Arabic), Dar Ul-Shorouq, Cairo, 1987, pp. 43–48 and 70–77.

[10] El-Naggar, S.: *Towards a National Strategy for Economic Reform* (Arabic), Dar Ul-Shorouk, Cairo, 1991.

[11] *ibid.*, pp. 39–42.

[12] Roe, A.R.: "Structural Adjustment and Productivity Growth", a paper presented to Cairo University Conference on *Productivity in the Egyptian Economy*, April 23–25, 1991.

productivity performance, namely, that (1) through price distortion it leads to the misallocation of resources, including the distortion involved in the over-evaluation of the exchange rate, (2) it deprives the domestic economy from the pressure to enhance productivity derived from international competition, (3) by producing for the narrow home market rather than a wide international market, it deprives the economy from productivity-enhancing investment, and (4) it reduces the availability of imported imports and spare parts which tends to reduce levels of capacity utilization. The author concludes that "a well-executed IMF package, while always painful if the initial disequilibrium is large, will nonetheless be less damaging to industrial and agricultural productivity than an adjustment based on the disorderly approach."[13]

5.3 *Unjustified Eclecticism*

While there is much to accept in the above diagnosis, one cannot help noting a persistent emphasis on certain factors, amounting almost to an obsession, while neglecting other factors which must have also contributed to the poor performance of Egyptian industry.

One of those factors not receiving sufficient emphasis is the relatively low share of manufacturing in total investment when compared with the share of nontradable goods and services. Throughout the forty years covered by Table 5.5, the share of the commodity sectors in total investment was less than 50%, which goes a long way to explain the predominant contribution of services to GDP growth shown in Table 5.1. With the exception of the 1960's, nontradables, together with petroleum, have absorbed more than two-thirds of total investment, and manufacture about a fourth. It is not a coincidence that the relatively greater contribution of manufacture to GDP growth in the 1960's was associated with a relatively greater share of manufacture in total investment. The decline in the share of manufacture in public investment as a result of the reorientation of economic policy after the launching of the open-door policy in 1974, has obviously not been compensated by a growth in the share of manufacture in private investment. This could be seen from Table 5.5, which shows a decline in the share of manufacture in total investment from 28% in 1974 to 22.7% in the 1980's, and also from Table 5.6 which

[13] *ibid.*, p. 7.

shows that between the first and second five-year plans of the 1980's, the decline in the share of manufacture in total public investment was not fully compensated by the rise in its share in private investment. As already noted in relation to agriculture, whatever encouragement may be given by economic policies to private investment in manufacture, the private sector may be lured by greater profitability elsewhere.

The poor performance of Egyptian industry is therefore not only a matter of low productivity of investment but has also to do with the magnitude of investment. The problem of low productivity also raises more issues than that of the relative efficiency of public and private enterprises. Incentives to management may be weaker in public enterprises but not necessarily the incentives to labour. The heavy hand of bureaucracy is certainly damaging to productivity, and corruption associated with administrative control could be immensely wasteful, but private enterprises have also their own forms of corrup-

TABLE 5.5
Gross Fixed Investment by Sector
(1952/3–1991/2)

(percentage)

Sector	1952/53 to 1959/60	1960/61 to 1964/65	1965/66 to 1966/67	1967/8 to 1973	1974	1975 to 1978	1978 to 1983/84	1982/83 to 1991/92
Agriculture, Irrigation & Drainage	12.9	22.9	21.8	15.8	7.6	7.5	7.7	7.1
Industry and Mining(1)	24.5	26.4	26.3	32.5	28.0	25.9	24.2	22.7
Petroleum	(a)	(a)	(a)	(a)	10.8	11.0	11.9	11.6
Electricity & Public Utilities	.9	10.3	19.9	12.5	8.9	7.9	11.6	17.0
Construction	(n.a.)	1.0(c)	1.3	.8	1.3	3.5	3.2	1.7
Transportation, Communication, Storage and Suez Canal	15.8	20.7	13.5	21.7	28.0	26.3	22.8	17.5
Trade and Finance	(n.a.)	1.1(b)	1.0	.8	1.3	1.3	2.8	2.3
Housing	29.5	10.9	12.2	10.8	7.6	10.1	8.8	10.9
Other Services(2)	9.0	6.9	3.8	5.0	6.4	6.6	7.2	9.2
Total	100	100	100	100	100	100	100	100

(1) not including petroleum after 1973
(2) including hotels and tourism
(n.a.) not available
(a) included in industry and mining
(b) four years only
(c) three years only
Sources: Calculated from Hansen, B.: *The Political Economy of Poverty* . . . , *op.cit.*, pp. 151–2 and from Ministry of Planning: *Preliminary Framework* . . . , *op.cit.*, vol. 3, p. 61.

TABLE 5.6
Changing Distribution of Private and Public Investment by Sector (between 1982/3–1986/7 and 1987/8–1991/2)

(percentages)

Sector	Public Investment		Private Investment	
	1982/3–1986/7	1987/8–1991/2	1982/3–1986/7	1987/8–1991/2
Agriculture	6.3	6.9	4.3	9.1
Manufacturing & Mining	24.1	19.7	23.2	25.5
Petroleum	4.4	2.1	25.7	23.3
Electricity & Energy	11.5	19.8	.2	–
Construction	2.2	1.5	1.7	1.8
Total Commodity Sectors	48.5	50.0	55.1	59.7
Transport, Communication, Storing & Suez Canal	27.9	24.6	7.9	5.0
Trade & Finance	1.7	1.6	3.5	3.0
Tourism	.8	.6	7.4	7.0
Total Productive Services	30.4	26.8	18.8	15.0
Housing	3.0	.8	24.0	24.1
Public Utilities	9.5	13.1	–	–
Education	2.7	3.6	.5	.4
Health	1.8	2.2	.7	.5
Other Services	2.6	3.5	.4	.4
Total Social Services	19.6	23.2	25.6	25.3
Total Fixed Investment	98.5	100	99.5	100
Change in Stocks	1.5	–	.5	–
Grand Total	100	100	100	100

Source: Ministry of Planning: *Preliminary Framework of the Third Five Year Plan*, 1991/2–1996/7), (Arabic) Vol. 3, pp. 67–71.

tive influences and waste which under certain political systems could be just as damaging to productivity and social welfare.

Reading the literature on the poor performance of Egypt's industrial exports, one gets the impression that there are unlimited opportunities to market them if Egypt could only produce large enough quantities of sufficiently high-quality products. While the problem could be more on the supply than on the demand side, demand factors are also involved. The relative success in raising the share of manufacture in total exports between 1950 and 1970 (Table 5.3) was not only the result of the rising share of manufacture in GDP until then, but was also partly a result of the favourable conditions prevailing in world trade during those two decades as well as the existence of a market ready to receive these exports in the eastern bloc. Increased protectionism in Western markets has harmed the manufactured exports of Egypt as it has harmed those of other Third World countries. The stagnation of Egypt's major manufactured exports (textiles) between the mid 1970's and mid 1980's, must have been partly due to the growing restrictions in Western markets on the textile exports of the Third World. The latest example of such restrictions on Egyptian exports of textiles is contained in a recent memorandum by the U.S. Department of State to the Egyptian government, in which it was claimed that Egypt's exports of ladies' and girls' woollen shirts and trousers, known in U.S. trade jargon as "category 448", were "creating disruption in the market for these products in the United States", and called for negotiations to fix a quota for exports in this category. In the same memorandum, it was claimed that "category 448" imports from Egypt reached 11,340 dozen from June 1992 to September 1992, which amounted to 3.5% of total imports in that category in the same period, and entered the U.S. at prices below those of American producers. The memorandum calls for limiting Egypt's exports of these products to 9,000 dozen per year, a reduction of about 75%.[14] It is often mentioned that the dependence of Egyptian exports of manufactures on the markets of the eastern bloc during the 1960's must have worked against raising productivity and improving quality, but it is important to add that those markets also provided greater stability and higher prices for Egyptian exports. To mention the former but not the latter aspect of this relationship with the eastern bloc is another example of unjustified eclecticism.

---

[14] *Al-Ahram Weekly*, 31 December, 1992.

5.4 *Indiscriminate Privatization*

Many of the causes of inefficiency and waste in the performance of Egyptian industry and exports of manufactures have more to do with certain macro-economic policies than with the system of ownership. Employment and pricing policies have created heavy burdens on public enterprises and contributed significantly to the decline in total factor productivity but are not themselves a necessary feature of public enterprises. Such policies could conceivably burden private as well as public enterprises and could be dismantled without abandoning public ownership of industrial firms. The damaging effects of these policies have indeed been less noticeable in the early days of nationalization than after the launching of the open-door policy. One explanation of this is that with the slowing down of the economy after 1965, and particularly with the growing difficulties after the 1967 war, including the need to cut down investment rates, the government seemed forced to throw greater burdens on public enterprises, burdens which would have been less necessary under more favourable circumstances.

In his recent book on the Egyptian economy, Professor Hansen recognizes that Egypt's economic growth "must have suffered substantially from the wars",[15] but seems to imply that investment, employment, pricing and foreign trade policies following the nationalization of the early 1960's are the main reasons for the decline in total factor productivity in industry after 1963/4, and hence sums up his discussion of the factors leading to this decline by saying that "public ownership may be the explanation."[16] But those policies of overstaffing public enterprises, starving them of investment funds and of the foreign exchange necessary to import spare parts and vital inputs, with the inevitable result of under-utilization of capacity and decline in total factor productivity, all these have themselves been part of the impact of the war conditions. Whether or not one considers these macro-economic policies to have been justified, they should not be attributed to public ownership *per se*. This is supported by the fact that total factor productivity in industry increased between 1973 and 1981/2 by 5% annually as a result of the greater availability of

[15] Hansen, B.: *The Political Economy of Poverty* . . . , p. 254.
[16] *ibid.*, p. 23.

raw materials and spare parts,[17] even though public ownership remained more or less intact during that period. In some of his earlier writings, Professor Hansen distinguished more clearly between detrimental macro-economic policies and the system of ownership. Thus, in an article published in 1975, he wrote:

> There is no indication that Arab Socialism should have been a vehicle for growth in the Egyptian economy. . . . The basic institutions, on the other hand, do not seem to be obstacles to growth and efficiency per se. The cooperative system in agriculture is known to be conducive to efficiency and growth under favourable conditions, and there is no reason why it should not be able to work in Egypt. And with public enterprises organized as joint stock companies, they should be able to function at least as efficiently as private joint stock companies. Both in agriculture and industry the inefficiency stems rather from investment and price policies adopted, the heavy-handed direct intervention from the side of the administration, and, more specifically, the administration of foreign trade. If market socialism were given a chance, it is the opinion of this author that efficiency could be restored within the present framework of ownership.[18]

Today's advocates of privatization in Egypt make no such distinctions. Wrong economic policies of all kinds, as well as all forms of wastes resulting from administrative inefficiencies or corrupted practices, even when such practices are initiated or supported by private foreign enterprises, are blamed on public enterprises and the invariable prescription is privatization. Successful public enterprises are lumped together with unsuccessful ones and losses are indiscriminately assumed to be avoidable only by privatization, even where it seems avoidable by providing incentives to managers of public enterprises and freeing them from strict administrative control. Privatization is also most commonly taken to mean a transfer of ownership even if privatization of management could do the job. The return to market forces is thus automatically interpreted as a return to private ownership. Considerations of profitability are taken to be paramount, whether what is involved is a department store which had been perhaps unduly nationalized, a hotel, a cinema, or a plant supplying many industries with some basic input and employing large numbers of labour. And in advocating a transfer of ownership from public to private, no distinction seems to be made between selling the enterprise to

[17] *ibid.*
[18] Hansen, B.: "Arab Socialism in Egypt", *World Development*, April 1975, p. 211.

Egyptians or foreigners. In either case, not only is it assumed that there will be gains in efficiency but it is also taken for granted that the impact on the balance of payments will always be positive.

5.5 *Indiscriminate Liberalization*

The real antithesis to import substitution is not export promotion but import liberalization. A country may pursue an import-substitution strategy and attempt to promote exports simultaneously, and one can be in favour of all sorts of measures designed to encourage exports but be wary of excessive liberalization of imports. We have already seen that Egypt's exports of manufactures improved and industrial output grew faster under the import-substitution strategy of the 1960's than under a much more liberal import system in the 1970's.

Liberalization of imports may be conducive to an increase in efficiency because of the pressure of competition, but it could of course kill the domestic industry before it has a chance to increase its efficiency. Whether or not this is a good thing reopens the whole issue of protection of infant industries which continues to be controversial. While the World Bank and the IMF, among others, are confident that import substitution has reached its limits in Egypt, Professor Hansen is not so confident. In his recent book, he writes that "while it probably is true that for manufacturing industry in Egypt, import substitution has been excessive, export promotion deficient and capital intensity excessive, hard evidence is not easy to find."[19]

Nor can the failures of many Egyptian industries to raise productivity and to reduce cost be attributed mainly to the lack of response to foreign competition. Foreign exchange as well as employment policies may have been more obstructive to raising efficiency in Egyptian industry than import restrictions. In fact, import liberalization has its own detrimental impact on efficiency if it leads to underutilization of capacity. To quote Bent Hansen again, "Sadat's Infitah, with its extensive import liberalization may be part of the explanation of the very high capital-output ratio for 1976 to 1980–81. Despite attempts by the government to protect public sector enterprises from the competitive onslaught by limiting own-exchange imports

[19] Hansen, B.: *The Political Economy of Poverty* . . . p. 160.

through special lists for commodities requiring licences, serious competition may nonetheless have been inflicted on both old and new public-sector enterprises, with low utilization of capacity the result."[20] The impact of import liberalization on capacity utilization is perhaps a mixed one, so that one cannot be certain whether the net effect is one of enhancing productivity in industry as a whole. Capacity utilization is increased by making imported inputs and spare parts more accessible but is decreased by narrowing the market as a result of competition from imported goods. Enterprises producing the less expensive varieties of industrial products and catering for the demand of lower-income groups may gain little from liberating the imports of inputs, since they rely more on local inputs, but suffer from the narrowing of the market as a result of the loss of that segment of demand which is now satisfied by imported goods, while having less access to export markets. The impact of foreign competition on these types of goods may therefore be higher cost and a further decline in quality. Recent reports indicate a big rise in the rate of under-utilization of capacity in a number of industries, including fertilizers, paper and other chemical products, as a result of the recent lowering of customs duties.[21]

But whatever may be the impact of import liberalization on productivity in industry, its impact on the balance of payments is even less certain. As it is with privatization, the expected increase in efficiency may very well be accompanied by an increase in the burden on the balance of payments as a result of unrestrained imports. The gain to the balance of payments from increased exports may be more than compensated by increased imports and repatriation of profits. Greater efficiency and higher rates of growth may therefore go hand in hand with a growing external debt. Twice in Egypt's modern history did greater economic liberalization leave Egypt more heavily in debt, as will be shown in the next chapter.

[20] *ibid.*, p. 526.
[21] Al-Ahram, 23 February 1993.

CHAPTER SIX

…RAL ADJUSTMENT AND EXTERNAL DEBT

6.1 *Summing up*

The twin policies of economic liberalization and privatization, presented to Egypt as the core of what is known as a "structural adjustment" program, are supposed to be the solution to virtually all of Egypt's economic problems, including low rates of growth of output, lopsided economic structure and growing balance of payments deficit. Perhaps the only problem that the advocates of structural adjustment are ready to confess its inability to solve is that of growing inequality. But even here, the solution is regarded as merely a matter of time. Structural adjustment measures may indeed be painful to start with to some particularly vulnerable groups of the population, but the benefits of rapid growth will sooner or later "trickle down" to them. Unemployment may grow as a result of privatization and the various measures designed to reduce the deficit in the government budget deficit, prices of some essential goods may rise and social services may suffer as a result of the elimination of government subsidies, but higher rates of growth are ultimately going to reduce unemployment and cutting down the budget deficit will ultimately reduce the rate of inflation.

The impact of structural adjustment on external debt is rarely discussed, but this is probably because it is taken for granted that structural adjustment would have a positive impact on the balance of payments and hence on the country's ability to service its debts. The need to contract new loans is therefore necessarily reduced.

Our survey in the previous chapters of the various factors that influence the balance of payments situation does not necessarily lead to the same degree of confidence that a structural adjustment program, as defined by the international finance institutions, provides a strong guarantee for reducing Egypt's external debt or against its future increase to the level prevailing before the recent exemptions. So many factors that work towards increasing indebtedness could continue to operate with or without structural adjustment and, more importantly, the structural adjustment program may bring with it other policies that contribute to an increase rather than a decline in external debt.

We have seen in Chapter One, that, at least since the early 1980's, private consumption has been more responsible for the decline in the rate of saving than government consumption, and that the rapid increase of private consumption may have been the result of a combination of sociological factors that economic policies of the kind envisaged by structural adjustment programs could be powerless to combat. Raising interest rates may discourage potential investors more than they restrain anxious consumers driven by an obsessive desire to emulate the higher consumption levels of higher income groups and to maintain their recently acquired social status. At least as important in causing government consumption to increase as the growth of government subsidies, which gets the greatest emphasis, are corruption and arms purchases which are often ignored or at least not part of the agenda of structural adjustment.

Whether structural adjustment measures necessarily lead to a reallocation of investment in favour of tradable goods and services and hence has a favourable impact on the balance of payments, has been shown by the discussions of Chapters Three, Four, and Five, to be by no means obvious. I have argued in Chapter Three, that our major sources of foreign exchange (oil, labour remittances, Suez Canal and tourism) are much more dependent on external circumstances than on deliberate measures taken domestically. Liberalization of agricultural prices and output policies may make private investment more profitable than it had been, but this may not be sufficient to compensate for the decline in public investment in agriculture. The same could be said about the impact of liberalization and privatization in industry. In any case, whether increased productivity and profitability in agriculture or industry will result in a reallocation of investment from nontradables towards these two sectors depends on relative profitability and hence on the impact of structural adjustment on profitability in other sectors as well. Structural adjustment may very well be associated therefore with a continuation of past trends, noticeable since the mid 1960's, of a decline in the share of agriculture and manufacturing industry in favour of services.

Whether private foreign investment would be forthcoming to a sufficient extent to reduce the need for borrowing from abroad depends, to a large extent, as we have seen in Chapter Two, on the balance of payments situation, and this, in its turn, depends on more

UNIV DUNELM

factors than those associated with structural adjustment. Egyptian exports are heavily dependent on fluctuations in international economic conditions, regional as well as domestic political fluctuations. But apart from the signals sent to potential foreign investors by Egypt's own balance of payments situation, whatever concessions Egypt may make to private foreign investment and whatever its efforts at implementing structural adjustment, foreign investors may be more tempted by other countries going through similar structural adjustment programs and offering greater rewards, like those of Eastern Europe, which will also be competing for concessionary external assistance.

All this may be dismissed as amounting to no more than saying that structural adjustment is not the only factor on which the future of Egypt's external debt depends, and no one would argue differently. More important therefore is the argument that structural adjustment programs tend themselves to be associated with factors that are not conducive to a reduction in the external debt burden.

Indiscriminate liberalization of imports and unlimited exposure to foreign standards of consumption are part and parcel of the policies associated with structural adjustment, and their impact on the balance of payments is by no means obviously favourable. Concessionary treatment of private foreign investment may lead to a greater outflow of foreign exchange in the form of repatriated profit and capital and greater import bill than the inflow of foreign exchange in the form of foreign investment and increased exports. If the distribution of income suffers as a result of the structural adjustment program, the impact on private consumption may be more adverse than is usually supposed. The net impact of greater inequality on the rate of saving may be negative since the higher propensity to save of the higher-income groups may be more than compensated by the greater pressure on the middle and lower-income groups to emulate the consumption standards of the rich, by increased corruption and by lower labour productivity. And "outward-looking" economic policy is also often associated with greater corruptive influence of foreign capital and greater leniency in tax collection. If in addition to all this, borrowing abroad is at least as much the result of an external pressure to borrow than of an internal need for foreign capital, one may also expect a greater readiness to succumb to such pressures in an environment that is more open to external influences than in a more "inward-looking" environment.

6.2 *Historical Evidence*

All this may be highly speculative, but not more so than the opposite line of argument which implies a guaranteed improvement in the external debt situation as a result of structural adjustment. The issue cannot obviously be settled either by mere logic, economic theory or statistical evidence. But our side of the argument may find further support in history. As was suggested at the end of the previous chapter, Egypt passed through two experiences during which greater liberalization of the economy was associated with the rapid growth of external indebtedness. The term "structural adjustment" was not used to describe the earlier shifts to a more liberal economic policy but it could have served just as well then as now had the habit of coining convenient labels of this kind been fashionable at the time. In both experiences, the main features of the new economic policies were basically the same as those constituting the more recent "structural adjustment": a much greater role for private enterprise, a much smaller role for government, a more hospitable climate for private foreign investment and a more liberal import policy. The first of these two earlier experiences was that separating the end of the reign of Mohamed Ali in the middle of the 19th century and the First World War, and the second fell between the launching of the open-door policy in the mid 1970's and the assassination of Sadat.

During the earlier experience (1848–1914), Mohamed Ali's system of state control, including his monopoly system, was abolished, imports and exports liberalized, private foreign investment generously treated and the system of private ownership of agricultural land firmly established. But while Mohamed Ali's reign ended with the country free of any trace of external debt,[1] in 1914, Egypt's external debt was greater than its national product.[2] In the more recent experience (1974–81), imports were again greatly liberalized after the severe restrictions of the 1960's, private foreign investment encouraged and state control of the economy greatly diminished, but Egypt's external debt grew much faster during those seven years than it ever did since the First World War. In both experiences, income did increase quite rapidly, but it was "growth with little development", if

[1] See Crouchley, A.: *The Economic Development of Modern Egypt*, London, Longmans, 1938.

[2] *ibid* and Marlowe, J.: *Spoiling the Egyptians*, Andre Deutsch, London, 1974.

by development is signified a desirable change in economic structure. One may also discern, in both experiences, a tendency for the pattern of income distribution to deteriorate as compared with the periods of greater state control, as will be shown in greater detail in the next chapter.

The association between greater liberalization and greater external debt may, of course, be a mere historical coincidence, but we have already suggested reasons why one may lead to the other. This interpretation may gain greater strength if one is to note that powerful external interests stood to gain from both Egypt's economic liberalization and the growth of its external debt. We have already suggested how this may have worked during the more recent experience of the 1970's[3] but there is no shortage of evidence on the 19th-century experience as well.[4] If history is any guide to the future, there are therefore good reasons to expect the coming period of "structural adjustment" in Egypt to be associated with another relapse into greater external debt.

6.3 *A Misuse of History?*

Advocates of structural adjustment do not make use only of economic theory and statistics but also of history, quoting the experiences of countries which applied structural adjustment programs with a relatively small debt burden. The experiences of a few countries in south-east Asia are thus repeatedly referred to as examples for other countries to follow. It is difficult to see, however, how a country like Egypt could hope to repeat, in the 1990's, experiences in which a number of extraordinary external circumstances combined to produce their success. Those countries, particularly South Korea and Taiwan, had relatively easy access to the wide and prosperous market of the United States at a period in which the U.S. was committed to much more liberal trade policies. The two countries were treated as frontline allies against communism and were thus provided with an Asian version of the Marshall Plan. "U.S. aid financed the equivalent of 95% of Taiwan's trade deficit in the 1950's. Economic aid to South Korea was even larger . . . (amounting to) between 1945 and

[3] See Chapter Three.

[4] See for instance, Marlowe: *Spoiling the Egyptians*, Andre Deutsch, London, 1974, and Landes, D.: *Bankers and Pashas*, Cambridge, Mass., 1958.

1978 almost as much as the total aid provided to all African countries during the same period. Another prerogative of frontline all ally-status was that the U.S. benignly overlooked the protected markets of Taiwan and South Korea, even as the IMF, the World Bank and GATT, . . . were telling the rest of the Third World to end their restrictions on imports. Finally, there was the Vietnam war, which was to the Taiwanese and South Korean economies what the Korean War was a decade earlier to the Japanese economy: a vital stimulus to economic take off."[5] Not only did the Vietnam war provide South Korea and Taiwan with an excellent opportunity in the form of U.S. purchases of agricultural and industrial goods and U.S. spending for "rest and recreation", but more significant were the Vietnam-related construction contracts which, by the end of the war in 1975, had accounted for almost 20% of Korean exports of goods and services.[6]

By the mid 1980's, however, the international environment had changed, with liberal trade policies giving way to increasing protectionism and the Third World countries finding it increasingly more difficult to market their exports. Apart from the fallacy of composition implied in expecting all Third World countries to realize similar gains to those achieved by a very few countries in south- east Asia,[7] the whole climate of world trade is very different from what it was when those countries had their success stories. In a lecture delivered in December 1979 in Stockholm, on receiving the Nobel Prize for economics, Arthur Lewis complained that economists repeatedly fall in the error of advocating a policy well after the passing of conditions in which it may have worked. Thus, in the 1940's and 1950's economists created a whole set of theories which made sense if world trade had been stagnant (e.g. balanced growth, regional integration, etc.) but which had little relevance in a world where trade was growing at 8% a year. "The fact that world trade was growing rapidly was not universally recognized until the second half of the 1960's. Then nearly every country discovered the virtues of exporting. Now we are in danger of being caught out again. Since 1973, the growth rate of world trade has halved, and nobody knows whether this is

---

[5] Bello, W.: *Brave New Third World: Strategies for Survival in the Global Economy*, Earthscan Publications, London, 1990, pp. 34–5.

[6] *ibid.*

[7] See Cline, W.R.: "Can the East Asian Model of Development be Generalized?", *World Development*, Vol. 10, February 1982, pp. 88–89.

temporary or permanent. But most of our economic writing continues to assume implicitly that a return to 8 percent is only just around the corner."[8]

Thirteen years after Arthur Lewis wrote this, his pessimism about world trade appears to have been fully justified. The international trade environment facing the exports of the Third World continues to be unfavourable, and with the increasing trend towards protectionism and trade wars in the developed countries, as well as their continued adherence to the objective of fighting inflation as having greater priority over rapid growth and full employment, "it would be rash to expect the 'locomotive of growth' which the industrial countries are to provide for the rest of the world to move fast in the next decade."[9]

6.4 *The Sacred Cow of Structural Adjustment*

Advocates of structural adjustment are unlikely however, to be dissuaded from the call for "export-promotion strategies" by any degree of pessimism about the future of world trade. Export promotion has become an article of faith, and it is precisely because it has become an article of faith that a revival of world trade continues to be believed to be "just around the corner"; the fact that what one or a few countries can get away with cannot be done by all countries at the same time, is ignored. One has to go back, in the history of economic thought, three or four centuries to come across a similar example of total surrender to an article of faith. But the similarities are striking. The mercantilist advocation in the 16th and 17th centuries of increasing exports as the primary goal of economic policy is

---

[8] Lewis, A. "The Slowing Down of the Engine of Growth," *American Economic Review*, vol. 70, September 1980, pp. 555–6.

[9] Singer, H.: "Beyond the Debt Crisis", *Development*, Journal of the Society for International Development, No. 1, 1992, p. 36. Professor Singer points out that in spite of the much-vaunted "outward orientation" of the 1980's, the rate of growth of exports of Third World countries has been disappointing. For low-income countries (other than China and India) this rate fell from 5.9% annually during 1965–68 to 0.5% in 1980–88. For lower-middle-income countries, the impact of outward orientation on export volume has been minimal, the increase being from 5.8% to only 6.0% during the two periods respectively. Only in the case of upper-middle-income countries and of Latin America has there been a significant increase in the *volume* of export but the terms of trade have deteriorated for both primary commodity and manufactured exports. *ibid.*

strikingly similar to today's obsession with export promotion. Economic activities were ranked then, as they are now, according to their ability to contribute to the balance of payments and to compete in foreign markets. Adam Smith's common sense remarks addressed against the mercantilist obsession with the accumulation of gold and silver, could just as aptly be addressed against today's obsession with export promotion.

But one may go further and search for similarities in conditions that could have led to our common folly. The Mercantilists were living at a time when new territories were discovered or conquered, new goods enjoyed and new tastes and consumption habits acquired. Today's obsession with export promotion has a similar foundation, even though new tastes are less voluntarily acquired and the consumption of new goods more forcefully urged. Foreign exchange is highly esteemed because of the high value attached to the ability to import. It is an article of faith that Third World countries cannot develop unless they import more, and their ability to develop is thought to be constrained mainly by their ability to import, not only capital goods but also technology, management and even value systems. It is mainly for this reason that an export promotion strategy is taken to be the only correct strategy. This is indeed the sacred cow of the development industry at present, which one dares to question only at one's peril. Behind it lies, not hard economic theory but a combination of ideology, value system and a specific way of understanding what development means. To challenge this orthodoxy requires no less than challenging the whole way of looking at the meaning and goals of development, but this would have taken us far beyond the goal of this essay.

CHAPTER SEVEN

THE PRESENT AS HISTORY

On reviewing the modern history of Egypt's economic policy, it is difficult not to note certain common features between the economic policies of the two best known of Egyptian leaders: Mohamed Ali (1805–1848), and Gamal Abdel Nasser (1952–1970). Though different in many other respects (think of their origin, the length of their reign, apart from the great differences between the economic and demographic conditions of the two periods), both leaders adopted strongly interventionist economic policies which, towards the end of their rule, turned the state into virtually "the sole manufacturer, the sole trader and the sole farmer". Of course, this last phrase contains some exaggeration, especially in the case of Nasser, but it is true that, in both experiences, the bulk of manufactured output, and of new investments in all sectors, came to be realized by the state, in addition to the very tight control by the state of prices, incomes and of the composition and marketing of agricultural output. It is worth noting, however, that this predominance of the role of the state was achieved, in the case of Nasser, mainly through nationalization, in contrast to the case of Mohamed Ali, where it was achieved mainly by creating what had not existed before, including the introduction of new and highly successful varieties of cotton.

This overwhelming role of the state was associated with three important economic features which to a large extent explain why these two periods stand out as constituting two of the most important turning points in Egypt's modern history. These three features are: 1) a radical transformation of economic structure in favour of manufacturing, (2) the achievement of a high degree of "economic independence", and (3) a significant rise in the level of living of lower-income groups.

Although these three statements should be interpreted cautiously and understood in relative terms, they seem to provide correct descriptions of some of the most important characteristics of these two periods, and in all three respects: economic structure, economic independence and income distribution, there was a clear deterioration during the two periods following the reign of Mohamed Ali and of Nasser respectively.

During most of the period falling between the end of Mohamed Ali's reign and the First World War (1848–1914), Egypt was ruled by weak, unambitious rulers who were strongly influenced or dominated by the representatives of foreign powers, even before the beginning of the British occupation in 1882. More important for the purposes of this chapter, is the fact that during the greater part of this long period, Egypt's economic policy was reoriented towards an open-door policy with regard to both foreign trade and foreign investment. The same thing could be said about the two decades which followed the death of Nasser in 1970. In both respects: the weakness and lack of vision of the rulers as well as the nature of economic policy followed, these two periods were in direct contrast to those of Mohamed Ali and Nasser, but so was the case also with regard to the three major features just referred to.

The aim of this chapter is to provide evidence for this allegation of striking contrast in these three respects between the Mohamed Ali/Nasser experiences on the one hand and the two periods of "open-door policy" which immediately followed them, on the other, and to present a tentative explanation of this contrast.

7.1 *Economic Consequences of Etatist Policies*

a. *Economic Structure*: The most obvious and least controversial of the economic consequences of the interventionist policies of both Mohamed Ali and Nasser was the radical change in economic structure. There are, of course, no national income statistics for Egypt under Mohamed Ali, but there is enough evidence that Mohamed Ali not only attempted but in fact succeeded in launching an industrial revolution in Egypt, through what Crouchley calls "an almost incredible effort of development".[1] Egypt was transformed from a country that produced hardly any manufactures other than the simplest kinds of textile, pottery, straw mats and sugar, to a country that produced, apart from textiles, spinning machines, weaving looms, armaments and every kind of ironwork. The modern factory system was introduced and by 1837, there were as many as 29 such factories all over

[1] Crouchley, A.: *The Economic Development of Modern Egypt*, London, 1938, p. 41.

the country. The cotton factories alone employed, in the 1820's, no less than 30,000 workers,[2] a stunning figure for a country of no more than 2.5 million people.

A similarly "incredible" and successful effort at changing Egypt's economic structure in favour of manufacturing was made by Nasser 130 years later. During the period of Nasser's and Egypt's first five-year plan (1959/60–1964/65), investment in industry and electricity was about 37.3% of total investment compared with 21% for agriculture (including the High Dam). Industrial output grew at 8.5% annually compared with 3.3% for agriculture, and employment in industry grew by 6.5% compared with only 3.3% for agriculture and 4.1% for total employment.[3] The share of manufacturing in GDP increased therefore, from 17% in1956 to 23% in 1965 and the share of industry, electricity and construction in employment, from 13% to 16% in the short period of five years 1959/60–64/65.

b. "*Economic Independence*": One is on less solid grounds arguing that there was a high degree of "economic independence" under both Mohamed Ali and Nasser, but only because the concept of economic independence is more elusive. Mohamed Ali certainly caused Egypt to be more integrated in the world economic system than it was before him, and as a result, Egypt came to be more "dependent" on external sources of goods than previously. It is a fact, however, that in spite of the great increase in the variety of goods available in Egypt under Mohamed Ali, imports were reduced to a minimum. To give one example, "a complete arsenal was erected with foundry, workshops, rope factory, etc., which could turn out everything required to make and fit out a complete ship-of-war except for the finer nautical instruments, brass nails and cannons, all of which were brought from England."[4] Needs have certainly multiplied, and so have imports; what is most impressive is the degree to which the growth of the former exceeded the growth of the latter. The point will become more readily accepted when the degree of economic independence under Mohamed Ali is compared, not with the much greater isolation of Egypt before 1800, but with the degree of dependence on imports that characterized the period following his reign, which

[2] Owen, R.: *Cotton and the Egyptian Economy: 1820–1914*, Clarendon Press, Oxford, 1969, p. 45.

[3] Hansen, B.: "Planning and Economic Growth in the UAR, 1960–65", in Vatikiotis, P.: *Egypt since the Revolution*, Allen and Unwin, London, 1968, pp. 22–35.

[4] Crouchley, *op.cit.*, p. 69.

is later referred to. To this must be added that, with all his efforts for development, Mohamed Ali left Egypt, as we have already seen, completely free from external debt, which is by itself an important indicator of economic independence.

With regard to the Nasserist era, it is important to distinguish between the years falling between the wars of 1956 and 1967, and the rest of Nasser's reign. The period 1956–67 could be rightly regarded as the most representative of Nasserist interventionist policies, for the earlier years (1952–56) were dominated by efforts to end the British occupation and the later years (1967–70) by the repercussions of the 1967 defeat. It is possible therefore to take the economic changes that occurred during this "interwar" period (1956–67) as constituting the real economic legacy of Nasserism. Table 7.1 provides 12 indicators of various aspects of "economic independence" related to foreign trade, including food imports, and the financing of investment. The figures show that with regard to almost all indicators related to foreign trade, the period (1957–67) achieved a higher degree of economic independence than the previous period (1952–56). This cannot be said of the burden of external debt since, as was already shown in Chapter One, Egypt was in fact a net creditor country before 1957 as a result of the accumulation of sterling balances during the Second World War, and started to accumulate increasing external debt afterwards with the rise in investment rate. It has also been shown in Chapter One, however, how the burden of external debt was made much lighter, up to the 1967 war, by the extremely soft conditions attached to during this period, both economically and politically.

c. *Income Distribution and Relative Poverty*: Several writers have drawn a picture of increased suffering under Mohamed Ali, both in the countryside and the towns. Not only do they refer to his incessant wars in Arabia, Sudan, Greece, Syria and in Turkey itself, but also to the forced labour of hundreds of thousands of peasants driven to work on his irrigation projects. Mohamed Ali's monopoly system is said to have been too harsh and exploitative, with the peasants being paid far less than international prices for their crops, which they were forced to deliver to the government. The peasants lacked incentives to grow cotton, which was particularly unpopular as it needed more work than other crops and brought little reward. Another source of complaint was the system of "solidarity" in tax payment, according to which, if one farmer failed to pay his taxes his

TABLE 7.1
Some Indicators of Economic Dependence

Period	Exports as % of Imports	Concentration of Exports(1)	Geographical Concentration of Exports (2)	Imports as % of GDP	Imports of Consumer Goods as % of Total Consumption Expenditure	Imports of Capital Goods as % of Gross Domestic Investment
1952–56	70	86	47	21	8	24
1957–67	70	75	39	21	5	22
1968–73	60	58	57	12	2	19
1974–80	80	69	58	24	9	26
After 1980	90(a)	84(b)	73(c)	35(d)	19(e)	32(f)

Period	Imports of Consumer Goods as % of Total Imports	Geographical Concentration of Imports(3)	Debt Service Ratio (4)	External Debt as % of GDP (5)	Foreign Financing as % of Gross Domestic Investment	Food Imports as % of Food Consumption (6)
1952–56	47	47	–	–	–	4
1957–67	38	58	10	26	15	4
1968–73	31	40	35	25	19	5
1974–80	35	62	26	48	32	34
After 1980	34(g)	79(h)	41(i)	53(j)	53(k)	41(l)

Notes:
(a) Average of 1981 and 1983/84.
(b) 1981–83 (c) 1983 (d) Average of 1981/82 and 1983/84.
(e) 1982 (f) Average of 1981/82 and 1982/83.
(g) Average of 1981 and 1982 (h) 1983.
(i) Average of 1982 and 1983 (j) Average of 1981/83.
(k) Average of 1981/82 and 1986/87 (l) 1983/84.
(l) Percentage of primary commodities in total commodity exports (2) Share of most important geographical bloc in total exports (3) Share of most important geographical bloc in total imports (4) Percentage of debt service to total exports of goods and services (5) Does not include military debt (6) Refers to 8 major food items: wheat, rice, maize, beans, lentils, edible oil, sugar and meat.

Source: Compiled from various tables in Issawi, I.: *The Measurement of Dependence in the Arab World*, (Arabic), Center for Arab Unity Studies and UN University, Beirut, 1989, pp. 138–201.

neighbours would be collectively responsible, and so was one village for the failure of another. Crouchley even refers to "the apathy and discontent" of industrial workers who were "dragged from their fields and workshops to labour in the factories".[5] Roger Owen describes the conditions of Mohamed Ali's industrial workers thus: "Working conditions were bad, hours were long, and there was every encouragement for the workmen to commit various acts of sabotage. St. John reported that there was not one of Mohamed Ali's mills which had not been accidentally or designedly set on fire".[6] Even if all this did not contain some element of exaggeration, it is very unlikely that the living conditions of most Egyptian peasants and industrial workers did not actually improve under Mohamed Ali. The change in this respect, brought about by Mohamed Ali as compared with what went on under the Mamlukes, is probably analogous to that brought about by the industrial revolution in England as compared with living conditions of the 18th century. Writers who describe the suffering brought about by the industrial revolution tend to forget the horrors of life before it. If Mohamed Ali did not pay the farmers the international prices of their crops, it was he in any case who allowed the country to make any benefit at all out of these crops, the most important of which were introduced by him. We also know that "the production of wheat, beans and barley remained fairly steady during Mohamed Ali's reign" and that in the 1840's, "cereal production rose to three or four times above its 1821 level."[7] People were almost certainly eating better, which at those times at least, was the most important measure of the standard of living. Demographic data lend support to this conclusion, since the population, which remained more or less constant during the first two decades of the century (at about 2.5 million), increased by no less than 75% between 1821 and 1847, to 4.5 million.[8] This increase occurred in spite of the high death toll resulting from the plague of 1845, which killed one-quarter of the population, in addition to the frequent wars.

The improvement in the standard of living of the lower-income groups and the narrowing of income gaps during the Nasserist era is less controversial. Those were the years (1956–1967) of the great expansion of the free or greatly subsidised social services of education,

---

[5] Crouchley, *op.cit.*, p. 72; see also Owen, R., *op.cit.*, p. 25.
[6] *ibid.*, p. 45.
[7] *ibid.*, pp. 49–59.
[8] Crouchley, *op.cit.*, p. 51.

health and housing and of the application and extension of land reform which put a ceiling on land ownership and land rents and provided valuable security for tenant farmers. Large industrial firms were nationalized, tax rates greatly increased on high incomes, profit sharing for industrial workers introduced and prices tightly controlled. Statistics show a significant increase in the share of wages in both agricultural and industrial incomes during the first half of the 1960's, a big increase in real agricultural and industrial wages during the same period, and an improvement in the distribution of consumption expenditure in rural areas as measured by the Gini coefficient.[9]

7.2 *Economic Consequences of Open-Door Policies*

Although the labelling of economic policy in Egypt as an "open-door policy" is only 20 years old, and was introduced to describe the shift in policies brought about by Anwar El-Sadat in 1974, this label can just as aptly be used to describe the shift which occurred in the mid-19th century, particularly under the reign of Said Pasha (1854–63) towards freer trade, greater foreign investment and less government control. The earlier experience of open-door policy lasted for almost a whole century, until the revolution of 1952, but important deviations from the open-door principle occurred during the three decades following 1914, largely because of war conditions and the world depression. The following discussion of the economic consequences of open-door policies will therefore be confined to the period falling between the end of Mohamed Ali's reign and the First World War (1848–1914), and the twenty years following the launching of Sadat's open-door policy (1974–1994). In all three aspects discussed in the previous section, the two periods witnessed remarkable deterioration.

a. *Economic Structure*: It is not an exaggeration to say that Egypt was a much less industrialized country in 1913 than in 1848. Rapid growth did occur in agricultural output and great progress was achieved in infrastructure, as indicated by the length of railway and telegraph lines introduced, the construction of roads and bridges, the digging of new canals, the expansion of sea ports and the opening of

[9] See Mabro, R. and Radwan, S.: *The Industrialization of Egypt, 1939–73: Policy and Performance*, Clarendon Press, Oxford, p. 170 and ILO, *Employment Opportunities and Equity in Egypt*, Geneva, 1982, pp. 95–6.

new schools. Most of this effort was done, however, to serve foreign trade and foreign investment and contributed little to the diversification of the economy. This was a period which could be described as one with "growth but little development". Although income statistics are lacking, the growth of agricultural production and international trade undoubtedly indicate a substantial increase in average income, but a much more unbalanced economy in 1913 than that which existed in 1848.

The similarity with the post-Nasser period is striking. Between 1975 and 1985 the annual rate of growth of GDP in Egypt was 8.5% in real terms, a rate which was rarely experienced in Egypt's modern history, and was surpassed only by very few countries during the same period. As a result, real per capita income more than doubled, from $334 in 1975 to $700 in 1985. Gross domestic investment was increasing at an unprecedented rate, reaching 25% of GDP in 1984, a rate 50% higher than the already respectable rate achieved during the period of comprehensive planning in the early 1960's. The most striking results of this high rate of investment were to be seen in the progress of infrastructure: transport and communications, electricity and natural gas, water and sewage systems.

Behind these successes, however, lies a much more bleak picture of failures and imbalances which were discussed at various points in earlier chapters: agriculture growing at a rate below that of population and well below that of GDP, and manufacturing growing at a much slower rate than services and crude petroleum. Thus, while the share of the two major "productive" sectors in GDP tended to decline, the share of extractive industries tended to rise. Between 1972 and 1985, the share of agriculture in GDP declined from 25% to 17%, that of industry (excluding petroleum) from 28% to 20% while the share of petroleum rose from 5% to 16% and that of services remained more or less the same at about 47%. The deterioration in the structure of employment was more serious, for while the share of manufacturing in the total labour force remained virtually constant at about 12% during that period, the decline in the share of agriculture was almost totally matched by the rise in the share of services in the labour force, which increased by about 50% (from 30% to 45%) and this is where "disguised unemployment" is most in evidence. The government sector, in particular, has been acting as the "employer of last resort", where those failing to find remunerative jobs in agriculture or manufacturing are employed at very low pay in return for little or no work.

This serious imbalance in economic structure has been quite effectively covered up for a considerable amount of time until it was dramatically revealed in the mid 1980's by the sudden collapse of oil prices. Between the mid 1970's and mid 1980's, the drastic increase in oil prices and in the oil revenues of the Arab oil-surplus countries opened new opportunities for work for hundreds of thousands of Egyptian labourers, both skilled and unskilled, who migrated to the Arab Gulf Countries and to Libya and sent back to Egypt what, in the early 1980's, became the largest single source of foreign exchange, surpassing even oil. The collapse of oil prices in 1986 revealed, however, how fragile the economic structure has been and how the rapid growth of income and infrastructure since the mid 1970's has been merely the result of regularly injecting the economy with external sources of income or capital, whether in the form of foreign aid, labour remittances or higher oil prices, all of which have little relation with an increase in productive activity at home.

b. *Economic Dependence*: According to virtually all the twelve indicators of economic dependence/independence contained in Table 7.1, Egypt became much more economically dependent during the period 1848–1914 than it was under Mohamed Ali. Foreign financing came to constitute a handsome proportion of domestic investment, while it played virtually no role under Mohamed Ali. Foreign debt emerged and grew until it constituted about 100% of national income at the turn of the century. Exports became even more dominated than ever by cotton, and both exports and imports became more concentrated in Britain. With the growth of the middle class and the increasing extravagance of the ruling elites, imports of consumer goods increased as a proportion of total consumption, and with the complete abandonment of capital-good industries, the imports of these goods must have grown as a proportion of total investment. The degree to which imports were covered by exports varied between the first half of this period (1848–1882), during which the deficit in current account tended to grow and was covered by increasing borrowing from abroad, and the second half (1882–1914) during which one of the main aims of the colonial administration was to realize a surplus on current account so as to service the foreign debt. Even with regard to self-sufficiency in food, the situation deteriorated in spite of the very rapid growth in agricultural production. With the increasing profitability and popularity of the cotton crop, cotton increasingly replaced wheat, and this, together with the increase in population, made the locally grown wheat insufficient, by the turn of the century, to meet the needs of the country. Imports of wheat and flour started to grow, which were again encouraged by the increasing availability of cheaper wheat from Canada, Australia and South America. By 1914, Egypt had become a British protectorate, had been under British occupation for over three decades, and was as politically dependent as it was economically.

Table 7.1 already provided data on the change in a number of indicators measuring "economic dependence" since 1974. It clearly points out the tendencies towards an increase in the concentration of exports, both with regard to their composition and their geographical destination, an increase in the geographical concentration of imports, the percentage of food imports in total food consumption, the proportion of foreign financing in domestic investment, the percentage of total imports in GDP, the percentage of imports of consumer goods in total consumption expenditure and in the percentage of imports of capital goods in domestic investment. Particularly striking is the growth of external debt, which has been discussed in greater detail in Chapter One.

c. *Income Distribution*: One can also confidently argue that income distribution must have worsened between 1848 and 1914, even though conclusive statistics are lacking. There are several indicators for this. In the first place, there was the emergence and growth of foreign ownership of agricultural land. While this was confined, under Mohamed Ali, to uncultivated land so as to encourage the reclamation of new land, foreigners were allowed by Khedive Said in 1858 to buy already cultivated land. Foreign ownership of agricultural land was confirmed under Ismail by a decree from Constantinople in 1867, and it went on growing with the failure of small cultivators to repay their debts to mortgage banks. In the second place, the burden of land tax became excessively high on small cultivators. What the small cultivator gained under Said, as a result of the abolishment of the "solidarity" principle in the collection of taxes, was lost under Ismail as a result of an excessively high burden of taxation to which Ismail was driven by his own heavy burden of foreign debt. The growing gap between the poor and rich under Ismail is vividly illustrated by Janet Abu-Lughod's description of the development of Cairo during his reign. She calls this development "a tale of two cities", these two cities being the modern part of Cairo which grew under the name of "Ismailia", between the Nile and the Azbakeya gardens, and was inhabited mainly by foreigners and the newly-rich Egyptians, and the "oriental" city which occupied roughly what is now called "Old Cairo", and in which the bulk of lower-income Egyptians dwelled. While this old "city" was left practically untouched, the new "city" was built in French style, all with pavements and boulevards lined with trees. This is to be contrasted with the Cairo of Mohamed Ali, the physical features of which was virtually the same when he died as when he came to power, except for the factories, iron foundries and the schools he built.[10]

The trend of growing inequality continued under the British occupation. The British can indeed boast of the big increase in Egypt's agricultural production, in the productivity and profitability of agriculture, in the security of land ownership as well as the reduction in the burden of taxation. But with this went a big increase in foreign ownership of agricultural land until it covered no less than one-seventh of total cultivated land by the turn of the century. The process of depriving small landowners of their land, which started under Ismail, also accelerated. The burden of land tax became indeed progressively lighter, but to a progressively smaller proportion of the population. By 1917 no less than 53% of the population of upper Egypt and 36% of the population of the Delta were landless.[11] More and more landowners were therefore forced to become either tenants of other people's land or merely agricultural labourers. For tenants, conditions became increasingly difficult with the growing scarcity of land, as agricultural rent tended to soar to the benefit of landlords. As for agricultural labourers, although they benefitted from the abolition of corvee labour, the more rapid growth of supply of labour compared with demand, especially with the migration every year of some 500,000 to 800,000 labourers from upper Egypt to the Delta, worked to keep the wage rate close to subsistence level.

The development of income distribution following the Nasserist era is less straightforward than the change in economic structure or in the degree of economic "dependence". Reviewing the various information and statistics available, one is left with a strong presumption that income distribution deteriorated slightly or remained more or less the same between the mid 1960's and the mid 1970's, both

---

[10] Abu-Lughod, J.: *Cairo: One Thousand and One Years of the City Victorious*, Princeton University, 1971.

[11] Owen, *op.cit.*, p. 240.

in the sense of the size of the gap between the rich and the poor and in the sense of the relative size of the population in absolute poverty. There are signs of significant improvement in the latter sense but a big deterioration in the former between 1975 and 1985, and of deterioration in both senses after 1985. The conclusion with regard to the period 1965–1975 is based on data on Gini coefficient,[12] on the development of real agricultural and industrial wages[13] as well as on the nature of economic policies undertaken during this period, which did not witness any important redistribution measures. This was also a period of economic stagnation following the 1967 war. The allegation of widening gap between rich and poor in the decade following 1975, is strongly supported again by the nature of economic policies followed during this period, the laxity of government efforts in collecting taxes and fighting corruption, and the very rapid growth of national income and external revenues. The suggestion that the proportion of people falling under the poverty line has declined in the decade following 1975 is supported by the ILO sample survey of rural Egypt in 1977, by statistics on the movement of real wages in both the rural and construction sectors[14] as well as by the study of the impact of the migration Egyptian labour abroad after 1975 on low-income groups.[15] The suggestion of a deterioration in income distribution since 1985, particularly in the sense of an increase in the proportion of people falling under the poverty line, is based mainly on the very big rise in the rate of inflation and in the rate of unemployment, and the big reduction in government expenditure on food subsidies and social services following the big fall in oil prices in 1986.

Looking at the period of the last 30 years as a whole (1965–1994), one is strongly inclined to think that the gap between rich and poor in Egypt has widened significantly since 1965, although the lower-income groups, especially in rural areas, may be living significantly better now than in the mid 1960's.

---

[12] ILO, *op.cit.*, pp. 93–96.
[13] Mabro and Radwan, *op.cit.*, p. 179.
[14] ILO, *op.cit.*, pp. 96–127.
[15] See Amin, G., and Awny, E.: *International Migration of Egyptian Labour*, IDRC, Ottowa, 1985, pp. 130–145.

7.3 *An Attempt at an Explanation*

It is, of course, possible that such associations as indicated above, between the degree of state intervention in the economy and certain economic and social features, may be no more than a coincidence, with no causal relationship involved. But one should not dismiss the matter as pure chance unless no causal relationship seems to be at all plausible. What follows is an attempt to find such a relationship.

Both Mohamed Ali and Nasser were committed to what may be called an "ambitious national project of independent development" to which they were strongly dedicated and for which they made a heroic effort to mobilize the nation's material and human resources. It was "ambitious" in the sense that the goals went far beyond what the country had achieved for a very long time before their rule, "national" in the sense that it revolved around the image of the nation's future rather than the ruler's own personal ambitions and involved almost every aspect of the country's development, and "independent" in the sense that it was not inspired or motivated by the interests of foreign powers, but rather was often in conflict with these interests. The two experiences may indeed have been "tolerated" by these powers but they were not "dictated" by them.

The nature of the two projects, though quite similar in many aspects, was by no means identical: military strength being the dominant element in the case of Mohamed Ali, in contrast to rapid industrialization and greater social justice in the case of Nasser. But in both cases, the fact that the project was highly ambitious and often came into conflict with the interests of foreign powers, seemed to require a high degree of consolidation of political and economic power in the hands of the state. The rapid change in economic structure was itself an essential element in Nasser's national project and was at least a necessary condition for the fulfilment of that of Mohamed Ali, since a strong army capable of fulfilling independent military targets required an ambitious industrialization programme. To increase the country's resources to an extent which would make possible the fulfillment of national goals, required a greater integration of the national economy into the international economic system, as was manifested by the growth in importance of foreign trade under Mohamed Ali, and of foreign aid under Nasser, but very clear and strict limits were drawn to this integration by the determination to preserve the ambitiousness and independence of the national project.

Hence all the elements of "economic independence" which were referred to above while describing both Mohamed Ali's and Nasser's experiences.

The implementation of this national project was bound to have important consequences, in both cases, for the standard of living and the way of life of the masses, both in the cities and the countryside. In the case of Mohamed Ali, the new irrigation projects, the introduction of new crops, the change in the system of cultivation and of tax collection, as well as the non-ending mobilization of new recruits for the army, radically changed the way of life of the peasants, and not always for the better. In the city, the introduction of the monopoly system, the massive industrialization programme, the restrictions imposed on merchants and craftsmen, the great expansion of education and the improvement of medical facilities, in addition to the successful maintenance of law and order, have also radically changed the way of life of the urban population, mostly for the better, and this affected a growing proportion of the total population. In the case of Nasser, life in the countryside was transformed by land reform and the various forms of government intervention in the production and distribution of agricultural output and agricultural income. In the city, life was transformed by redistribution measures, industrialization, the growth of bureaucracy and army, and the expansion of education, medical, and other services. In both experiences, economic progress was achieved at the cost of political authoritarianism. This probably did not entail great sacrifices in the earlier experience, except for the human sacrifices entailed by Mohamed Ali's military campaigns. The political price was much higher in the Nasserist experience, and the controversy will probably go on forever regarding whether or not the economic benefits of Nasserism were greater than its political cost.

In both cases, the transformation of the way of life of the masses, more often than not for the better, was not dissociated from the high degree of independence, attempted and achieved, from foreign pressure. Lacking a permanent and reliable source of foreign support, Nasser had no alternative but to rely on a domestic source of support which, given his attack on the old ruling elite of big landowners and urban bourgeoisie, could only be provided by the lower ranks of the middle class, industrial workers and small landowners. In this way, a relationship could be seen between the commitment to an independent national project and the third feature of the

Nasserist era: the improvement in the standard of living of the lower-income groups. One may note a similar relationship between Mohamed Ali's pursuing of an independent project and his new reliance on a purely "Egyptian" army consisting, for the first time in centuries, of Egyptian peasants.

It is important to emphasise that this commitment to a "national project of independent development" was conspicuously lacking in the two extended periods that followed the two experiences of tight state control under Mohamed Ali and Nasser. Successive rulers between the end of Mohamed Ali's reign and the First World War were mostly weak and unambitious, and/or severely manipulated by foreign powers. The same thing could be said of the rulers following Nasser. Whether this was merely a historical accident or the inevitable result of the prevailing international or domestic conditions is, of course, a highly controversial issue.

7.4 *A Guide to the Future*

In almost all aspects of economic policy, the Mubarak regime, which followed the assassination of President Sadat in 1981, has been essentially a continuation of that of Sadat. Whether in their attitude towards private foreign investment, to foreign trade policy or to the role of government in the national economy, including their attitude towards income distribution, both the 1970's and 1980's stand in direct contrast to Nasserist interventionist policies of the 1960's. This is as true of official declaration of policy as it is of actual implementation, so that it is not wrong to view the main function of the economic policies of the 1970's and 1980's as the dismantling of the Nasserist economic legacy. It is important, however, to note the slackening down of the process of economic liberalization during the first half of the 1980's. Whether in trade liberalization or in the extension of new concessions to private foreign investment, the early years of Mubarak look like an interruption of a process started by Sadat in 1974. The process was again resumed in 1987, and accelerated after the signing of new agreements with the IMF and the World Bank in 1991. "Structural Adjustment" measures, which were taken rather timidly and hesitantly before 1987, were now taken persistently and with much greater force.

It is interesting to speculate on the possible reasons for this suspension of the process of economic liberalization between 1981 and 1987. What seems utterly futile is to try to look for an explanation in possible ideological differences between the two Egyptian presidents or among those taking top policy decisions, since such differences, if they exist at all, have accounted for very little over the last two decades. The two major events that occurred around 1986 and could have some bearing on the acceleration of economic liberalization, were the big fall in oil prices early in 1986, and the beginning of the end of the Cold War. The fall in oil prices, by drastically reducing Egypt's foreign exchange revenues and national income, may have made the Egyptian government much easier to manipulate by its creditors as well as by the international financial institutions. The ending of the Cold War may have also allowed these institutions, as well as the U.S. government, a freer hand in shaping national economic policies in the Middle East as elsewhere.

If Egypt's earlier experiences in economic liberalization following periods of tight government control, are to be used as a guide to what the future might bring, once could come up with the following fairly plausible predictions. Higher rates of growth of output may be realized if no new external shock is to occur, such as another big fall in the prices of oil or a revival of terrorist threats giving another blow to tourism. But the hoped-for change in economic structure, resulting from a faster growth in agriculture and manufacturing than in services, and even the continuation of the improvement in the balance of payments, look much less certain. As far as economic structure is concerned, the actual result will depend on the relative attractiveness of agriculture and manufacturing to potential investors, as compared with such sectors as tourism, trade, finance and oil. With regard to the balance of payments, the future will depend on the net impact of liberalization of imports and export promotion efforts, as well as on the future trend of external debt. As was argued earlier, there is nothing to guarantee that the liberalization of trade and investment will have a beneficial impact on the balance of payments in the long run, and there are already signs that Egypt is returning again to the bad habit of relying on external borrowing. We have seen the same thing happening twice before in modern Egyptian history, and there is no reason why liberalization will now have different results. But the most likely negative impact of the implementation of structural adjustment is its impact on the living standards of lower-income groups.

7.5 *Structural Adjustment and the Poor*

In a recent World Bank report,[16] 20–25% of the total population of Egypt were classified as "poor", about half of them (10–13%) being described as "ultra poor". In rural areas, the poor include the landless, very small landholders and agricultural labourers, while in the cities they include most workers in manufacturing and services and a significant number of government employees. The ultra poor include widows, and the older, sick and disabled people who heavily depend on direct income transfers.[17]

Already before 1987, a good percentage of the population, but particularly those classified as "poor", must have suffered from the early applications of "structural adjustment" measures, but mainly from the successive reduction of government subsidies to some essential goods and services. Real wages in the public sector in 1987 were 90% of what they were in 1973, while real wages of government employees fell by 50% during the same period.[18] Between 1982 and 1987, the cost of what is called "minimum cost diet" increased by 216% in urban areas and by 242% in rural areas.[19] Since the Egyptian poor are estimated to spend 75–80% of their income on food, their only response to higher food prices is to reduce their food consumption. In fact, according to the same World Bank report, "some recent evidence suggests that the majority of households have been decreasing their food consumption in response to these food price increases."[20]

With the acceleration of structural adjustment measures after 1987, the state of the poor must have deteriorated further. Subsidies to various basic items were further reduced or eliminated including that given to "Balady bread" which accounts for 50–60% of the calories in the lowest income households, raising its price by 150% in one year (1989). Several rationed food items such as beans and lentils were taken off the ration/subsidy system, while reducing the quantities and raising the prices of other rationed items such as rice, sugar, edible oil and tea. Water and electricity tariffs as well as the price of

---

[16] World Bank: *Egypt: Alleviating Poverty during Structural Adjustment*, Washington D.C., 1991.

[17] *ibid.*, p. XIV.

[18] *ibid.*, p. 95.

[19] *ibid.*, p. XVII.

[20] *ibid.*, p. 106.

kerosine, which is widely used in cooking by lower-income groups, were also subject to successive increases since 1987. Government expenditure on social services, as a percentage of GDP, declined from 5.9% in 1984/5 to 4% in 1990, while government expenditure on education per student in the late 1980's was about one-fifth of what it was ten years earlier, in real terms.[21]

Although the process of reducing government subsidies has gone a long way, it is by no means completed. The prices of electricity and petroleum products are planned to be brought up to international price levels by 1995, and government expenditure on health and education is planned to be reduced further. More serious perhaps is the expected impact of the process of privatization, which has just started, on the rate of unemployment, as well as the impact of a drastic reduction in the number of redundant employees in government services where overstaffing has been estimated in the 1970's to be as high as 40%.[22] The unemployment rate is already as high as 20% of the labour force and is significantly higher among university graduates.

No one is denying that structural adjustment has caused and will continue to cause hardships, particularly for those who are already poor, but it is usually alleged that the pain is only temporary and that everyone will stand to benefit from the reform program in the long run. This optimism is based on the view that once the interference with prices and restrictions on the free play of market forces are abolished, the serious misallocation of resources which has characterized the Egyptian economy since the 1960's, is also going to end, and private investment, both national and foreign, will be encouraged, boosting up the rate of growth of output and employment. Export promotion will open new employment opportunities in the export-oriented industries, including small-scale labour-intensive industries in which Egypt may have comparative advantage. The freeing of interest and exchange rates from official control will also encourage the use of labour-intensive techniques allowing greater absorption of those seeking employment. All this will take time before it brings relief to the poor and the unemployed, so that some measures may have to be taken to alleviate the temporary hardships. Much hope is attached and great publicity is given to the newly

---

[21] *ibid.*, pp. 113 and 117.

[22] *ibid.*, p. 46.

established "Social Fund for Development", which has the declared aim of alleviating the short-term adverse effects of privatization, by creating new employment opportunities and retraining displaced labour.

But there is much to be sceptical about, both in the short-term measures suggested and in the optimism about the long-run benefits to the poor. The total resources promised to the Social Fund for Development by the aid donors, amounted to $610 million at the beginning of 1992, when the Fund started its operations. However, what was available to it, to spend during its first year of operations, did not exceed $34 million. Even if all the promised resources were made available, and if all of these were actually spent on creating new employment opportunities without any administrative expenses or any expenditure on project identification and project appraisal, and estimating the cost of creating one new job at L.E. 10,000, no more than 200,000 new jobs would be created. This is no more than half the number of new entrants in the labour market every year. Even if the impact of the Fund is measured in relation only to the unemployment created by privatization, it still appears to be quite limited. Surplus labour in 116 public enterprises has recently been estimated at 600,000 persons, to which must be added the high percentage of redundancy in government services which has already been referred to.

There are also good reasons to suspect that the resulting hardships will not be only temporary. The success or failure of the proposed program of reform will ultimately depend on its success or failure in creating sufficient opportunities for productive employment. But the optimism of the advocates of structural adjustment is based, not only on their belief that private investment is better in doing this than public investment, but also on the belief that this is going to more than compensate for any loss of employment opportunities resulting from reducing public investment. This is far from being obvious. Apart from the brief period of the late 1970's and early 1980's during which large-scale external migration took place and greatly reduced the pressure on the labour market, open unemployment has been growing regularly since the early 1980's with the progressive liberalization of the economy. The increase in private investment, national and foreign, has not made up for the fall in the share of public investment. Between 1977 and 1987, private national and foreign investment created together about 1.5 million jobs, and of these, 145,000 jobs have been created by private foreign investment, i.e., less than 10% of the total.[23] Compared with the increase in the number of those seeking employment, this is a very modest contribution. Recent experience in this respect does not therefore provide grounds for optimism, and greater liberalization in the future even if it proceeds at a much faster rate than in the early 1980's may not bring any better results. Much more important than administrative interference in interest or exchange rates or in the labour market by imposing a minimum wage, as a cause for discouraging the use of labour-intensive techniques, may be the nature of the goods produced, the size of the firms producing them, the nature of the market in which the goods are sold, and even certain characteristics of the consultants who prepare the feasibility studies. There are very narrow limits, for example, on the use of more labour-intensive techniques by a multinational firm producing a luxury good in Egypt, for sophisticated high-income consumers, in Egypt or abroad. Much more seems to be required, to absorb the unemployed in new and remunerative jobs, than merely to allow the free play of market forces.[24]

7.6 *Structural Adjustment and Human Development*

Advocates of structural adjustment sometimes go further and allege that their program for reform is necessary, not only for raising the material standard of living of rich and poor alike, but also for the fulfillment of a more wholesome life as implied by the term "human development" which has been newly adopted by U.N. agencies. Such, for example, is the message of a recent report published by the Institute of National Planning in Egypt with the technical co-operation of the United Nations Development Programme.[25]

---

[23] Handoussa, H.: "Egypt's Investment Strategy: Policies and Performance since the Infitah", in Al-Naggar, S. (ed.): *Investment Policies in Arab Countries*, (Arabic), Arab Fund for Economic and Social Development and the Arab Monetary Fund, Kuwait, 1989, p. 365.

[24] Shortly after the signing of the May 1991 agreement between the IMF and the Egyptian government, the Director-General of the IMF was addressing Egyptian businessmen and high-level officials in Cairo, when he was asked how long did he expect the period of tightening belts would last in Egypt. His frank reply was that there was no near end in sight for the tightening of belts. His reason was that just as Egypt is entering the race of economic readjustment, other Third World countries are doing the same. The competition is therefore going to be tough.

[25] Institute of National Planning: *Egypt: Human Development Report, 1994*, Cairo, 1994.

The report defines "human development" (HD), simply as "a process of enlarging people's choices,"[26] which hardly goes beyond the familiar goal of economic growth, since any increase in the quantities of goods and services produced would necessarily enlarge somebody's range of choice. This is the case irrespective of how necessary the good is or who gets it. The enlargement of people's choices is indeed the argument used by Arthur Lewis forty years ago while defending economic growth in the sense of a mere increase in goods and services.[27] The report frankly rejects the basic needs approach to development on the grounds that it results in an inferior type of development, or what it calls "development of a second degree compared with that of the North". In contrast, "HD is concerned with the satisfaction of all needs—basic or non basic. Given that HD is a process of enlarging people's choices, the distinction between basic needs and luxurious needs is redundant as a normative prescription."[28]

"Human development" is regarded as consisting of three components: life expectation at birth, adult literacy rate and real per capita income,[29] so that a country would be considered more successful than another in "human development" if it has a higher life expectation, a greater literacy rate among adults and a higher per capita income, or a "higher" combination of these three components. But these three components or indicators hardly take us any further than the traditional measurement of development as the mere increase in the quantities of goods and services available per head. The third component is the familiar measure of growth while the first component, namely, life expectation at birth, is more a measure of the length than of the quality of life. There are, in any case, other members of the animal kingdom which live longer than man without having an index similar to that of "Human Development" or having the technical co-operation of a UN agency. Expectation of life at birth does, of course, reflect, to some extent, the state of health and nutrition, but there are so many aspects of the diet and health conditions that may cause suffering and a strong sense of deprivation, without necessarily reducing the expectation of life at birth. The opposite is also

---

[26] *ibid.*, p. 4.

[27] Lewis, A.: *The Theory of Economic Growth*, Appendix: "Is Economic Growth Desirable?" Allen and Unwin, London, 1955.

[28] *ibid.*, p. 6.

[29] *ibid.*

true, so that expectation of life at birth may show significant improvement with no significant improvement in health conditions or in the level of nutrition. A big reduction in infant mortality, for example, could be achieved over a very short period of time, leading to a significant increase in the expectation of life at birth without any improvement in other important aspects of the quality of life. This has been very much the case of Egypt, where, between 1970 and 1987, life expectation at birth rose by as much as 16 years for the country as a whole (from 46 to 62 years) while many important indicators of the quality of life, such as housing conditions, the quality of education, transportation, air and water pollution, etc., have deteriorated. Similar remarks could be made about the second indicator, namely, adult literacy rate, which seems to be a better measure of labour productivity than of "human development". A society can become more literate while leading a progressively "less human" existence. Many more variables must be at stake where genuine "human development" is involved.

One such variable is the pattern of income distribution, since it reflects not only the degree to which some basic needs are satisfied, but also the degree of social tension and frustration that grow with the growth of inequality. Income distribution does not appear, however, as one of the components of human development adopted by this report. In fact, the report adopts the all-too-familiar view that the improvement in the standard of living of the poor depends primarily on raising the rate of growth of GDP. This is nothing but the old "trickling down" theory which makes it necessary, in order for the poor to become less poor, that the rich should become richer in the first place! The report tries to support this view by quoting the experiences of some countries where the poor may indeed have benefited from faster growth, while ignoring the experiences of other countries where this did not take place. It also reads the Egyptian experience in a way that could lend support to this view by pointing out that periods of rapid GDP growth in Egypt, such as the two periods of 1959–64 and 1974–80, were also periods of improvement in income distribution. But this ignores the fact that the earlier period was also a period of strong government intervention in favour of lower-income groups, and the second was a period of a very high rate of migration. The authors of the report are, of course, anxious to show that the coming era of structural adjustment, by raising the rate of growth of GDP, must also be good for the poor. It follows that the alleviation of the plight of the poor does not need more government intervention on their behalf. In fact, the report boldly alleges that the Egyptian poor will benefit from less public expenditure on education, health and housing, as well as from the abandonment of a minimum wage since "minimum wages or rigid wage structures tended to discourage enterprises from providing vocation-specific skills training, that would otherwise be paid for by employees through reduced wages."[30] The welfare state is described as "no more than an illusion, justifying the violation of the humanity of people by barely satisfying their essential needs".[31] The best way to improve the living conditions of the poor is neither the welfare state nor the basic needs strategy, but rather, "outward focused development strategies" which "emphasize competition in product and factor markets to encourage efficiency in production".[32] Thus, structural adjustment turns out to be not only the best strategy for rapid GDP growth and increasing material wealth, but also for something called "human development". But alas, this "human development" turns out with little scrutiny to be only another name for the same old principle of economic liberalization and the free play of market forces.

[30] *ibid.*, p. 70.
[31] *ibid.*, p. 5.
[32] *ibid.*, p. 70.

CHAPTER EIGHT

ECONOMIC CHANGE, SOCIAL STRUCTURE AND RELIGIOUS FANATICISM

Side by side with the economic changes that occurred in Egypt over the last three decades and were described in the previous chapters, including the transformation of economic policy, economic structure, external economic relationships, and income distribution, Egypt witnessed an important transformation of its social structure. This was manifested mainly in the rapid growth and changing characteristics of the "middle class". Many of the economic and social problems associated with Egypt's development over the last thirty years could be traced to this transformation of social structure, which in turn is closely associated with the changes in economic policy. This chapter will investigate the possible relationship between the change in Egypt's social structure and the widely discussed problem of growing religious fanaticism.

8.1 *The New Middle Class*

In trying to justify his "socialist" measures of the 1960's, the late Egyptian President, Gamal Abdel-Nasser was fond of describing the Egyptian society on the eve of the 1952 revolution as "the half percent society", meaning that the proportion of the Egyptian population that controlled most of Egypt's resources as well as its political life did not exceed that tiny percentage. This may have been an exaggeration but probably a slight one. The statement also implied a very small middle class and its relatively weak position, economically and politically.

Some idea of the smallness and weakness of the Egyptian middle class in the early 1950's could be obtained from a 1955 estimate contained in a British government report of income distribution in Egypt. According to this estimate, 1% of the total Egyptian population had an annual income per family of more than L.E. 1500, compared with less than L.E. 240 for 80% of the population. The remaining 19% of the population, constituting the "middle class", had, therefore, an annual income ranging between L.E. 240 and 1500 per family.[1] Out of the total population of Egypt in 1952, of 21.4 million, about 200,000 persons could therefore be regarded as constituting the "higher class", 4 million as constituting the "middle class" and more than 17 million, as belonging to the "lower class". This is not inconsistent with what we know about the distribution of agricultural land ownership in Egypt in 1952, when about 2000 families owned about one fifth of all agricultural land and about 2 million families (or about half the Egyptian population) owned less than 2 *feddans* per family.[2]

Social stratification cannot obviously be based on the same criteria 40 years after the 1952 revolution. Landownership can no longer be regarded as the decisive factor as it was then, since other sources of large incomes have become more important. Higher education is also no longer a main feature of members of the middle class, since several new sources of high income do not require high educational achievement. With the high degree of social mobility that characterized the last forty years,[3] affiliation to certain families is no longer a necessary or sufficient condition for belonging to the "higher" social strata. "Westernization" or the ability to adopt western patterns of behaviour, lost much of its importance in distinguishing one social class from another as a result of the spread of these patterns of behaviour among the lower classes, as well as the rise in social status of sections of the population that have relatively little contact with the West. While income and wealth continue to be important criteria for classifying the population into the three social classes, the nature and the source of income and wealth have lost much of their importance in this classification compared with forty years ago.

Making use of a variety of data contained in the 1986 population census, of various estimates of the proportion of the Egyptian population falling under the poverty line, and of indicators of income distribution revealed by recent Family Budget Surveys, one may tentatively suggest a level of income of L.E. 300 per month per family in 1990 as the border line between the "lower" and "middle" classes,

---

[1] See Issawi, Charles: *Egypt in Revolution*, Oxford University Press, Oxford, 1963, p. 118 and p. 156.

[2] See Barakat, A.: *Ownership of Agricultural Land between Two Revolutions 1919–1952*, (Arabic), Ahram Centre for Political and Strategic Studies, Cairo, 1978, p. 61.

[3] See Amin, G.: "Migration, Inflation and Social Mobility", in Tripp, Charles and Owen, R.: *Egypt under Mubarak*, Routledge, London, 1989.

and of L.E. 10,000 as the border line between the "middle" and "higher" classes. According to this classification, about 53% (or 30 million people) of the 56 million, constituting the Egyptian population in 1990 would belong to the "lower class", about 45% (or 25 million people) would constitute the "middle class" and the remaining 2–3% (1–2 million persons) would constitute the "higher class".

The two figures below are meant to illustrate the change that occurred in the relative sizes of the three classes over the last forty years. In Figure la, the ratios between the three classes, based on the data for 1952 referred to above, are 1:20:85, while the ratios for 1990 illustrated in Figure 1b are 1:17:20. According to these two classifications, the middle class would have grown in size more than six times in the last 40 years while the lower class would have grown by only 75%, and the higher class five to ten times.

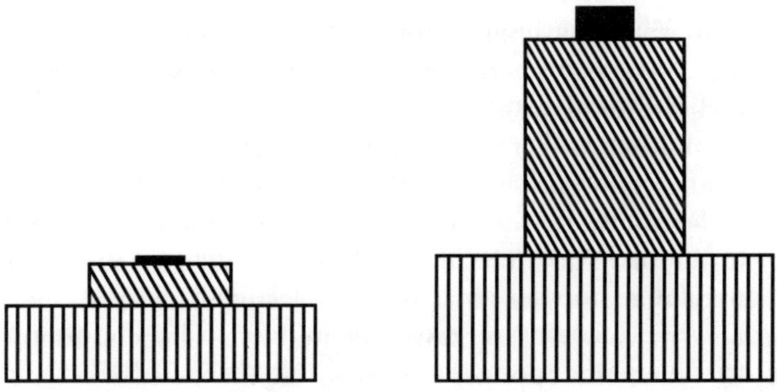

Figure 1a Figure 1b

But no less important than the change in relative size has been the change in the characteristics of the three classes. The new higher class does not consist mainly of the descendants of the older higher classes, but rather of families of recently acquired wealth, whose fortunes have accumulated mainly during the 1970's and 1980's, since such an accumulation of wealth would have been possible only rarely before the launching of open-door policies. The main sources of the new wealth were trade, particularly import trade, contractor activities, speculation in land, and commissions of all types. "Intermediate activities" of all kinds were thus the major source of newly acquired wealth and income, in contrast to the main source of income for the older higher class, namely, the ownership of agricultural land. The new middle class includes, like the older middle class, professionals, merchants, the higher and middle echelons of government officials, owners of middle-sized and small manufacturing firms, holders of middle-sized farms and owners of urban property. In addition, the new middle class includes some elements or descendants of the older "higher class" who have fallen in relative status as a result of the various measures taken by the revolution such as confiscation of property, nationalization, sequestration, etc. But most importantly, the new middle class now includes, in contrast to the old middle class, a good proportion of craftsmen and of the higher echelons of employees in private and public sector industry. The lower class now includes, as in the past, landless farmers, small landholders, low-income craftsmen, petty traders and most of agricultural and industrial labour, but it now also comprises a good proportion of the lower echelons of government and public sector employees.

Needless to say, the average income of all three classes is significantly higher than it was 40 years ago. The lower class is living, on the whole, much better than did the lower class of the pre–1952 years and their conditions of health and nutrition have definitely improved, while the other two classes are also enjoying much higher incomes than they did in the early 1950's. This does not necessarily mean that the lower or middle classes are less frustrated or more satisfied with their lot than the lower or middle classes of the pre-revolution days. In fact, in view of the unprecedented rate of social mobility of the last 40 years, the opposite seems to be the case.

8.2 *Social Mobility, and Economic Frustration*

A good proportion of Egypt's "new middle class", no doubt exceeding 50% and maybe as high as 75%, consists of what may be called "lower middle class", where monthly income per family does not exceed L.E. 600. This lower middle class includes the great majority of the low and middle ranks of employees in the government and industrial enterprises, the majority of public sector workers and retail traders as well as a good proportion of those working in private sector manufacturing firms and small agricultural landholders. There are good reasons to believe that a high proportion of those belonging to this lower middle class have been suffering most of the last two decades from a growing sense of frustration, dissatisfaction with their lives, loss of self respect and a grudge against the society at large. The symptoms are numerous, including the increasing rate of certain types of crime, which include crimes against close relatives, the rise in the number of emmigrants and of applications to emigrate, increasing corruption at various levels of government, increasing break-ups of families and other symptoms captured more in literary production than in social research. Possible explanations for this increasing frustration are also numerous but most of them are bound up with the rising rate of social mobility. The sudden and big increase in opportunities for increasing income and accumulating new wealth which were associated with the launching of the open-door policies in the mid 1970's, the opening up of new remunerative opportunities in the Gulf countries as well as the sudden rise in the rate of inflation, have whetted the appetite of a large section of the population but caused great frustration among those who, for one reason or another, failed to benefit from the new opportunities. When the economy started to slacken in the early 1980's and particularly following the big fall in oil prices in 1986, with the resulting decline in work opportunities in the Gulf countries, many of the rising aspirations built up in the 1970's were suddenly seen to be unrealistic and a strong feeling of frustration followed. The big increase in the rate of unemployment during the second half of the 1980's, reaching, according to some estimates, 20% of the labour force (an unusually high rate for Egypt) and considerably higher rates among university and intermediate college graduates, must have intensified the feeling of disappointment among large sections of the population who attached great hopes on educational achievements for themselves or for their children, as a channel for social advancement.

In a book originally published in 1927, the prominent sociologist P. Sorokin presented an interesting thesis which may throw important light on a number of changes in social behaviour which emerged in Egypt over the last two decades including growing religious fanaticism. According to Sorokin,[4] in situations where social structure is relatively stable, the lower classes tend to imitate those patterns of behaviour which are associated with the higher classes, but the opposite seems to occur in periods of rapid social mobility when the

---

[4] Sorokin, P.: *Social and Cultural Mobility* (1927), The Free Press of Glencoe, Illinois, 1959, pp. 565–8.

declining classes are inclined to adopt many of the values and behaviour patterns associated with the lower but rising social groups. There are good reasons to believe that this may be true. There is, first, the greater self-confidence acquired by the rising classes resulting from their economic success and allowing them a greater degree of self-assertion. Secondly, there is the sheer spread of their numbers, again resulting from their greater income, making their presence felt to an unprecedented extent in schools, universities, clubs and other public places which have for long been the protected privileges of the higher classes. Thirdly, there is the increasing infiltration by these rising classes of mass media, resulting from their increased access to education and allowing them to spread their habits of thought and social values to the whole society. Exactly the opposite developments become the fate of the declining classes whose influence gradually recedes with the decline of their self-confidence vis-à-vis their new rivals and their gradual withdrawal from public life. Willingly or unwillingly, but often unconsciously, they come to accept and even adopt the new patterns of behaviour and even the moral values of the lower classes, and discard their own.[5]

If our present estimate of the magnitude of growth of the middle class in Egypt is at all close to the truth, the sheer rise of the new middle class, and particularly of the lower ranks of this class, would add strength to the possibility that such influences have been at work in Egypt during the last few decades. If to this one adds the new causes of frustration and unfulfilled aspirations since the early 1980's, one may be very close to an understanding of the growth of religious fanaticism. A growing tendency towards the stricter observance of religious teachings carried by the rising sections of the population with a very modest social and educational background, can easily turn into religious fanaticism if met with severe disappointment of earlier hopes of social advancement. It is striking how rare it is to find examples of religious fanaticism among either the higher or the very lowest social strata of the Egyptian population. While members of the higher class are obviously exempt from the frustration brought about by a feeling of inferiority, members of the lowest social strata are saved from this frustration by their realization of the near impossibility of changing their relative social status. It is also interesting to note the differences between the expression of religiosity of these social

[5] Amin, *op.cit.*, pp. 117–8.

groups and that of the lower middle class, where one finds not only many more examples of fanaticism, but also an obviously greater degree of hypocrisy which could be the result of the same cause, namely, the frustration of unfulfilled ambitions.

Both recent research as well as studies of earlier parallel experiences, tend to support this conclusion. In his pioneer study of militant religious movements in Egypt, Saad Eddin Ibrahi[6] found that of the 34 militants studied who had participated in the attack on the Military Academy in 1974 or belonged to the militant religious group named *al-Takfir wal-Higra*, twenty-one, or about two-thirds, were sons of government employees, mostly in middle grades of the civil service, four were sons of small merchants, three were sons of small farmers (owning between six and eleven acres) and two had working-class fathers. With regard to educational level, 19 of the fathers had intermediate education and only seven had university degrees. According to Ibrahim, "it is safe to conclude that the class affiliation of most members of these militant Islamic groups is middle and lower middle class. It is also clear from the results of this study that the educational and occupational attainments of most of the members of these groups were decidedly higher than those of their parents,"[7] which indicates an upwardly mobile social strata who may easily consider their actual attainments considerably less than what they had originally hoped for or than what they deserved.

Tackling a much earlier period of Egyptian history, Albert Hourani has reached similar conclusions in connection with the growth of the Muslim Brothers' movement in the late 1930's, pointing out that it was "spreading in the urban population—among those in an intermediate position: craftsmen, small tradesmen, teachers and professional men who stood outside the charmed circle of the dominant elite."[8]

8.3 *The Rentier Class and Religious Fanaticism*

Not only failure, but success could also be a source of religious fanaticism. Just as it could provide an escape from the frustration created by the failure to realize one's material ambitions, it could also

[6] Ibrahim, S.E.: "Egypt's Islamic Militants", in Hopkins, N. and Ibrahim, S.E. (eds.): *Arab Society, Social Science Perspectives*, American University in Cairo Press, Cairo, 1987, originally published in *MERIP Reports*, no. 103, 1982.

[7] *ibid.*, p. 503.

[8] Hourani, A.: *A History of the Arab Peoples*, Faber and Faber, London, 1991, p. 349.

provide a useful cover for an accumulation of wealth or income that are either illegal or immoral.

We have already seen how, following the rise in oil prices of 1973/74, Egypt witnessed a period of unprecedented increase in income. Between 1973 and 1984, the average annual rate of growth of GDP was 8.5%, which was surpassed by very few countries, and real per capita income almost doubled. But we have also seen how very little of this increase in income was due to the growth of commodity sectors other than oil. Agriculture was growing at a rate well below that of population growth and manufacturing grew at a much slower rate than services and crude petroleum. The major contributors to this rapid growth of income were oil revenues, labour remittances, the Suez Canal, tourism and foreign aid.[9]

The structure of employment showed a similar imbalance in favour of the service sectors. During the period of most rapid growth (1977–1984/85), employment in agriculture increased by no more than 9%, employment in manufacturing and mining by 38%, and in all commodity sectors by 20% compared with an increase of services by 45%.

Egyptian economists have for a long time been warning against the economic dangers of excessive dependence on such unreliable sources of income and employment that are subject to factors largely outside Egypt's control, less amenable to policy manipulation and more sensitive to political changes. But there are also good reasons to believe that there may be a strong relationship between the growth of incomes that have the nature of economic rent and the growth of religious fanaticism.

The growth of unproductive activities, and of some incomes that are largely dissociated from effort, seem to provide fertile ground for the growth of irrational habits of thought. Income and wealth that grew at unprecedented rates are more likely to be explained by "God's blessing" than regular and slow improvements that can be more easily traced to one's own productive effort. Productive activities allow much less leisure for the idle speculation of religious fanatics. Religious fanaticism could also be an alternative source of self-esteem which is no longer provided by the productivity or usefulness of one's work. But most important of all seems to be the use of religiosity as a cover for illegal, immoral or undeserved income and wealth. Not

[9] See Chapter Three above.

only may religious pretence create the impression of deservedness of income and wealth but it could also be a very effective smoke screen to hide forbidden or socially unacceptable behaviour. The larger the undeserved commission or the bribe, or the monopoly price charged from the consumer, or the divergence from the safety requirements of building a block of flats, or from the legal requirements of obtaining an import license, or of benefitting from government subsidies, the greater the degree of pretence of being a good muslim. Some writers have suggested that the fact that so many Egyptians have spent some years during the 1970's and 1980's in the Gulf countries where religious tenets are more strictly observed, may have contributed to the growth of religious fanaticism in Egypt. It seems much more likely that such copying of other people's pattern of behaviour cannot become so widespread unless there is sufficiently fertile soil for its proliferation, and what is suggested here is that such a soil was provided by the unproductive, rentier nature of the Egyptian economy during the last two decades. The fact that the decade of the 1960's witnessed much less religious fanaticism but also fewer symptoms of a rentier economy, may not be a sheer coincidence.[10]

The relationship between the growth of a "rentier economy" and the growth of religious fanaticism in Egypt may be best illustrated by the emergence and growth of the so-called "Islamic Investment Companies" during the 1980's, already referred to in Chapter Three. As we have seen, these companies managed to mobilize billions of dollars of the savings of Egyptians from their earnings in the oil countries, and competed very successfully with commercial banks in mobilizing labour remittances, by offering considerably higher interest rates (often double that offered by the banking system) through calling it profit rather than interest to comply with the popular interpretation of Islamic principles. Apart from appealing to religious sentiments and offering a higher financial return, this phenomenon

[10] Egyptian social and cultural life have also witnessed the appearance of figures who played a prominent role in the mass-media and had wide popular appeal, who were strongly reminiscent of Moliere's "Tartuffe", a phenomenon with hardly any parallel in the 1960's. The combination of Tartuffe's false religiosity and materialistic greed seems to flourish more in certain social environments than in others and it is well-known that Moliere's "Tartuffe" was a straightforward comment on an important social phenomenon at the time. There is also some evidence to suggest that the "Tartuffes" of late 17th century France were largely to be found among a new, recently enriched "rentier" class. (See for instance, Lough, L.: *An Introduction to 17th Century France*, Longman Green Co., London, 1954, pp. 41–42.)

could also be seen as a fascinating example of the impact of a high rate of social mobility on economic behaviour, of which we have already met other examples.[11] Certain features of these companies and of the way they operated seem curiously to fit with certain features of the savings invested in them and the nature of the activities and aspirations of those who realized those savings. Having made a big jump up the social ladder through migration to the oil-rich countries, or achieved other windfall increases in income and wealth, and anxious not to lose the newly-acquired social status, investors in those companies found the high returns on investment, even though of dubious origin, greatly welcome. When the sources of the newly-acquired income and wealth are themselves highly suspect, the secrecy provided by the Islamic Investment Companies were particularly welcome as well as, one may add, the religious cover-up provided by them. When the increase in one's income or wealth is of dubious origin, one may be quite satisfied with an explanation of the profit realized and distributed by these companies, as being "God's blessing," as these companies, actually maintained. Investment companies of this type, with their religious pretentions, may therefore be much more understandable in an era of rapid growth of incomes that have the nature of rent, than in more stable times when more incomes are realized from productive activities.

It goes without saying that rapid social mobility, growing frustration among social groups with unfulfilled ambitions, or the growth of a rentier class whose increasing income and wealth are largely divorced from effort, could only be *some* of the factors that contributed to the growth of religious fanaticism. Other factors must be involved and could be important, including possible external influences with or without material support. But it also goes without saying that whatever the role of the external influences, they would be powerless if the domestic economic and social environment did not make such a large section of the population so receptive.

---

[11] See Chapter Two above.

REFERENCES

Abdallah, H.: *The Economics of Energy in Egypt* (Arabic), Academy of Scientific Research and Technology, Cairo, 1992.

Abu-Lughod: *Cairo: One Thousand and One Years of the City Victorious*, Princeton University, 1971.

Amin G.: *Food Supply and Economic Development in Egypt*, Cass, London, 1966.

———. *The Modernization of Poverty*, Brill, Leiden, 1974.

———."External Factors in the Reorientation of Egypt's Economic Policy" in Kerr, M., and Yassin, S., *Rich and Poor States in the Middle East*, Westview, L.A., 1981.

———. *The Arab East and the West*, (Arabic), Center for Arab Unity Studies, Beirut, 1979, 1983.

———."Adjustment and Development: The Case of Egypt", in El-Naggar, S. (ed.): *Adjustment and Development Strategies in the Arab World*, IMF & AMF, Abu Dhabi, 1987.

———. *The Story of Egypt's External Debt* (Arabic) Ali-Mukhtar Publishing House, Cairo, 1987.

———. "Migration, Inflation and Social Mobility", in Tripp, Charles and Owen, R. (eds.): *Egypt under Mubarak*, Routledge, London, 1989.

Amin, G. and Awny, E.: *International Migration of Egyptian Labour*, IDRC, Ottowa, 1985.

Barakat, A.: *Ownership of Agricultural Land between Two Revolutions 1919–1952* (Arabic), Ahram Centre for Political and Strategic Studies, Cairo, 1978.

Al-Beblawy, H.: *Change for the Sake of Stability* (Arabic), Dar Ul-Shorouq, Cairo, 1992.

Bellow, W.: *Brave New Third World: Strategies for Survival in the Global Economy*, Earth Scan Pubications, London, 1990.

Butter, D.: "Debt and Egypt's Financial Policies" in Tripp, Charles and Owen, R.: *Egypt under Mubarak*, Routledge, London, 1989.

Central Agency for Auditing: *Report on Egypt's External Indebtedness on 30 June 1984 and Policies Affecting it*, (Arabic), not dated, (mimeo.).

Central Agency for Public Mobilization and Statistics. *Statistical Yearbooks*.

Central Bank of Egypt: *Annual Reports*.

———: *Monetary and Credit Situation During 1990/91* (Arabic), September 1991.

Chinweizu: "Debt Trap Peonage", *Monthly Review*, November 1985.

Cline, W.R.: "Can the East Asian Model of Development be Generalized?" *World Development*, February 1982.

Commander, S.: *The State and Agricultural Development in Egypt since 1973*, Ithaca Press, London, 1987.

Condliffe, J.: *The Commerce of Nations*, Norton, N.Y., 1950.

Crouchley, A.: *The Economic Development of Modern Egypt*, Longmans, London, 1938.

Dethier, J.: *Trade, Exchange Rate and Agricultural Pricing Policies in Egypt*, World Bank Comparative Studies, 1989.

Dodwell, H.: *The Founder of Modern Egypt: A Study of Mohamed Ali*, Cambridge (U.K.), The University Press, Cambridge (U.K.), p. 1931.

Economist Intelligence Unit: *Country Reports: Egypt*.

Egyptian Economic Society: *Proceedings of the 50th Anniversary*, Cairo, 1960, (Arabic).

Esfahani, H.: *The Experience of Foreign Investment in Egypt under Infitah*, Faculty Working Paper, College of Commerce and Business Administration, University of Illinois at Urbana-Champaign, December 1990.

Al-Gabaly, M.: "The Road to Agricultural Development" (Arabic), *L'Égypte Contemporaine*, April 1981.

———.: *A Modern Look at Agriculture in Egypt*, (Arabic) Dar Al-Taawon, Cairo 1984.
Al-Gritly, A.: "The Structure of Modern Industry in Egypt," *L'Égypte Contemporaine*, Dec. 1947.
———.: *Economic History of the Revolution: 1952–66*, (Arabic), Dar El-Maaref, Cairo, 1974.
Handoussa, H.: *15 Years of U.S. Aid to Egypt*, a paper submitted to the 13th annual symposium, Center for Contemporary Arab Studies, Georgetown University, April 14–15, 1988 (mimeo.)
———. "Egypt's Investment Strategy: Policies and Performance since the Infitah", in Al-Naggar, S. (ed.): *Investment Policies in Arab Countries*, Arab Fund for Economic and Social Development and Arab Monetary Fund, Kuwait, 1989.
———. "Reform Policies for Egypt's Manufacturing Sector", in Handoussa, H. and Potter, G.: *Employment and Structural Adjustment: Egypt in the 1990's*, A.U.C. Press, Cairo, 1991.
Hansen, B.: "Planning and Economic Growth in the U.A.R.: 1960–65", in Vatikiotis, P. (ed.): *Egypt since the Revolution*, Allen and Unwin, London, 1968.
———. "Arab Sociolism in Egypt", *World Development*, April 1975.
———. *The Political Economy of Poverty, Equity and Growth: Egypt and Turkey, A World Bank Comparative Study*, Oxford University Press, Oxford, 1991.
Hansen, B. and Marzouk, G.: *Development and Economic Policy in the UAR (Egypt)*, North-Holland, Amsterdam, 1965.
Hasan, P.: "Structural Adjustment in Selected Arab Countries", a paper presented to the symposium on *Adjustment Policies and Development Strategies in the Arab World*, organized by IMF and AMF, Abu Dhabi, 16–18 February 1987.
Hussein, A.: *The Egyptian Economy from Independence to Dependence, 1974–79* (Arabic), Dar El-Wehda, Beirut, 1981.
Ibrahim, S.E.: "Egypt's Islamic Militants", in Hopkins, N. and Ibrahim, S.T. (eds.): *Arab Society: Social Science Perspectives*, American University in Cairo Press, Cairo, 1987.
Ikram, K.: *Egypt: Economic Management in a Period of Transition*, John Hopkins University Press, Baltimore, 1980.
Institute of National Planning: *Egypt: Human Development Report, 1994*, Cairo 1994.
International Monetary Fund: A.R.E.: *Recent Economic Developments*, June 19, 1984 (mimeo.)
———: *Report on Recent Economic Developments in Egypt*, January 1990 (mimeo.).
Issawi, Charles: *Egypt in Revolution*, Oxford University Press, London, 1963.
Issawi, I.: *The Measurement of Dependence in the Arab World* (Arabic), Center for Arab Unity Studies and UN University, Beirut, 1989.
Al-Khawaga, L.: *The Return of Egyptian Migrant Labour from Arab Oil-Producing Countries and its Impact on the Egyptian labour market* (Arabic), Center for Economic and Financial Studies, Faculty of Economics, Cairo University, Cairo, 1989 (mimeo.).
Landes, D.: *Bankers and Pashas*, Cambridge, Mass., 1958.
Lewis, A.: "The Slowing Down of the Engine of Growth", *American Economic Review*, September 1980.
Mabro, R.: *The Egyptian Economy*, 1952–72, Clarendon Press, Oxford, 1974.
Marlowe, J.: *Spoiling the Egyptians*, Andre Deutsch, London, 1974.
Mead, D.: *Growth and Structural change in the Egyptian Economy*, Richard Irwin, Illinois, 1967.
Middle East Economic Survey.
Ministry of Planning: *Preliminary Framework of the Third Five-Year Plan*, 1992/3–96/7 (Arabic).
Mitchell, T.: "America's Egypt: Discourse of the Development Industry", *Middle East Report*, March–April 1991.

Myrdal, G.: *The Challenge of World Poverty*, Allen Lane, The Penguin Press, London, 1970.
Al-Naggar, S.: *Towards a National Strategy for Economic Reform* (Arabic), Dar Ul-Shorouq, Cairo, 1991.
National Bank of Egypt: *Economic Bulletin.*
Roe, A.R.: "Structural Adjustment and Productivity Growth", a paper presented to Cairo University Conference on *Productivity in the Egyptian Economy*, April 23–25 1991.
Sadowski, Y.: *Political Vegetables?*, the Brookings Institution, Washington D.C., 1991.
Shehata, I.: *A Program for Tomorrow* (Arabic), Dar Ul-Shorouq, Cairo, 1987.
Singer, H.: "Beyond the Debt Crisis", *Development*, (Journal of the Society for International Development), No. 1, 1992.
U.S. Embassy in Cairo: *Egyptian Economic Trends.*
World Bank: *World Debt Tables.*
——— : *World Development Report.*
——— : *Trends in Developing Economies.*
——— : *A.R.E.: Economic Prospects and External Capital Requirements*, March 22, 1977 (mimeo.)
——— : *A.R.E.: Issues of Trade Strategy and Investment Planning*, January 1983.
——— : *A.R.E.: Current Economic Situation and Growth Prospects*, October 1983.
——— : *A.R.E.: Country Economic Memorandum, Economic Readjustment with Growth*, September 1988.
——— : *A.R.E.: Economic Redjustment with Growth*, 1990.
——— : *Egypt: Alleviating Poverty during Structural Adjustment*, 1991.
Zaki, R.: "The External Debt Issue", in Abdel-Khalek, G. (ed.): *The Open-Door Policy: Its Roots, Harvest and Future* (Arabic), Arab Center for Research and Publishing, Cairo, 1982.
——— : *Studies in Egypt's External Debt* (Arabic), Madbouli, Cairo, 1985.

INDEX

UNIV DUNELM

DURHAM UNIVERSITY LIBRARY
3 0104 00826832 2